THE MIGHTY ACT OF GOD

THE MIGHTY ACT OF GOD

An Adult Study Text

By Clifford A. Cole

herald house

Independence, Missouri

Christian Education Commission
Reorganized Church of Jesus Christ of Latter Day Saints

Library of Congress Cataloging in Publication Data

Cole, Clifford Adair, 1915-
The mighty act of God.

"Christian Education Commission, Reorganized Church of Jesus Christ of Latter Day Saints."
1. Jesus Christ—Person and offices—Study.
2. Christian education—Text-books for adults—Reorganized Church of Jesus Christ of Latter Day Saints. I. Reorganized Church of Jesus Christ of Latter Day Saints. Christian Education Commission. II. Title.
BT207.C65 1984 232 84-594
ISBN 0-8309-0393-3
Printed in the United States of America

To my wife, Lucile, whose quiet faith and love have sustained me and have been the better part of our mutual witness for Jesus Christ.

CONTENTS

And the same word was made flesh, and dwelt among us, and we beheld his glory, the glory as of the Only Begotten of the Father, full of grace and truth.—John 1:14

A PERSONAL PREFACE

Probably more books have been written about Jesus Christ than about any other person. Being aware of this, I wondered about my ability to write anything that has not been expressed more insightfully by other writers. I have learned, however, that I must bear my witness, and that the Holy Spirit calls and empowers me to be a blessing to others as I share my faith.

In this book I attempt to express my faith about the meaning of the most amazing act of history—the Mighty Act of God in Jesus Christ. There are no adequate human words to describe how God entered into the temporal universe in the person of Jesus of Nazareth. This text, therefore, does not set forth some fresh idea. Rather it is my faith statement distilled from a lifetime given in ministry with others. I hope that the Christ who is the subject of the book uses my human limitations, as he has so many times in the past, to open the hearts of those who share the witness. May this book contribute to the Saints' ever-growing understanding of the meaning of God's presence among the members of the body of Christ.

I acknowledge with appreciation the help of my wife, Lucile, who is always my kindest critic and the source of my greatest encouragement. Shirley Juliff and Grace Andrews have contributed greatly by giving many hours in typing the manuscript.

Walter Duty, L. D. Harsin, and Evelyn Maples carefully edited the manuscript providing a more concise and effective statement of my faith in Jesus Christ.

Paul Edwards and Walter Duty prepared the study helps for each chapter. These offer assistance in applying my thoughts to the reader's life situation.

* * * * *

All Bible quotations are from the Holy Scriptures (Inspired Version) unless otherwise noted. Versification differences may occur if another version is used.

Clifford A. Cole

CHAPTER

THE CREATOR SPEAKS TO CREATION

How shall we, as human beings and more specifically as Latter Day Saints, speak of God? He has been called Creator, Alpha and Omega, Omnipotent, Father, Lord, and a host of other names. The theologian Paul Tillich spoke of God as the Ground of Being. All of these words fall far short of expressing even a limited grasp of what is meant when people say "God."

In some measure we can understand the dilemma felt by the Apostle Paul when he wrote, "I knew such a man, (whether in the body, or out of the body, I cannot tell; God knoweth;) how that he was caught up into paradise, and heard unspeakable words, which it is not lawful for a man to utter" (II Corinthians 12:3, 4). While this scripture may indicate that the man was forbidden to repeat the words he had heard, it is clear that he could not find a way to communicate thoughts which were beyond the comprehension of his hearers.

We often find it difficult to expand our minds to grasp understandings beyond our experience. When I was taking an elementary course in college physics, the professor explained the principles involved in separating sunlight into its spectrum of colors. He then startled the class by saying, "The shortest band of light rays you can see is the violet. Now tell me, if you could see the next band shorter than the violet, what would its color be?" After some looks of amazement were exchanged, a student volunteered, "I think it would be more violet than the violetest violet we ever saw."

"Why would you think that?" the professor questioned. "The red band is the longest light wave we see, but shorter bands don't get redder than the reddest reds; they go into orange and yellow and green."

In modern parlance such thought "blows your mind." Many minds have not encountered such things and have no way to imagine them.

This problem is most apparent when talking about God or subjects related to God. We are always pushed beyond any human experience. As a result, our minds are unable to grasp such thoughts. Sometimes we have hints and intimations of things beyond temporal existence but we have no words to adequately communicate the idea.

One of these unfathomable ideas of faith is the concept of God. Most of us agree with an expression of God as creator. When we say God is creator we generally mean that he has brought into being all that exists in this universe. God has caused everything in "space" to be, and has created it in the sequence called "time." In this sense we live in a universe of time and space which we believe has been created by God. These are not only created by him, they may also, by his action, pass away or cease to exist. Therefore it can be said that time and space are temporal—subject to living and dying, being formed and passing away, existing and ceasing to exist. In the Doctrine and Covenants it is written:

> And the Lord God said unto Moses, For mine own purpose have I made these things. Here is wisdom, and it remaineth in me. And by the word of my power have I created them, which is mine Only Begotten Son, who is full of grace and truth. And worlds without number have I created, and I also created them for mine own purpose; and by the Son I created them, which is mine Only Begotten. And the first man of all men have I called Adam, which is many.
>
> But only an account of this earth, and the inhabitants thereof, give I unto you; for behold there are many worlds which have passed

away by the word of my power; and there are many also which now stand, and numberless are they unto man; but all things are numbered unto me; for they are mine, and I know them.—Section 22:21

The temporal universe is, therefore, subject to time and may end in time. The idea of the end of time is another of those concepts that are hard to grasp. We use such phrases as "the end of the world" (Matthew 24:4; 28:19), "time is no longer" (Doctrine and Covenants 83:17b), or "for the former things are passed away" (Revelation 21:4). Since the concepts are overwhelming and only partially comprehended, we tend to speak of them poetically as a matter of faith rather than as scientific facts.

We find it most difficult to push the mind into thoughts which go beyond or outside the temporal universe of time and space. Since God is the creator of time and space he is more than, and not limited to, time and space. He was before his creations and is more than his creations. God would continue even if that which he creates ceased to exist. He continues to be God.

The Eternal Contrasted with the Temporal

That dimension of God which is outside of the temporal is called eternal. We cannot describe the eternal in terms which are used to discuss the affairs of time and space, but there are few other words. *Eternal* is a difficult word to use. People tend to give it such time-related meanings as "endless" or "forever." Such meanings are inadequate because *eternal* cannot be defined in terms of time. It deals with that which is beyond or outside time and space. In reality it means that which is of God. God is eternal. Life with God is eternal.

We often disagree about the nature of God or of things eternal because we are limited in thought and language to our temporal universe. We want to attribute to God many of the characteristics and boundaries which we experience. We try to place God or the things of God in a location; we say "Heaven is up," "God sits on a throne," or "God must look like a man because Adam was made in God's image."

When engaged in such thought we may be doing the only thing possible. God is experienced through the Holy Spirit as "person." The highest image of "person" we can imagine is a human being. It is therefore understandable that we think of God in such a manner.

Even so, humility leads to realizing that God is not limited to human concepts. It is always appropriate to understand, as did the Apostle Paul, that

> we know in part, and we prophesy in part. But when that which is perfect is come, then that which is in part shall be done away. When I was a child, I spake as a child, I understood as a child, I thought as a child; but when I became a man, I put away childish things. For now we see through a glass, darkly; but then face to face; now I know in part; but then shall I know even as also I am known.—I Corinthians 13:9-12

Even though we now can only know "in part," it is our faith that we are destined to know more fully when we participate with God beyond time.

Ways to Learn About God

God is revealed through his creations. We understand something of his greatness as we search for the outermost limits of the universe. We learn about the Creator when we study the intricacy of God's handiwork in the minutest component of an atom. We see something of his love of beauty in a buttercup or the majesty of a mountain. We have confidence in the order and dependability of God in the operation of natural law. All of these speak about God.

We know something about God through prophets who have experienced the Holy Spirit. As the prophets wrote or spoke under the influence of the Holy Spirit, literature was produced that became scripture. By reading those scriptures we have some confrontation with the divine. We know about God through the ministry of the prophetic leaders of the world.

Many of us have experienced the ministry of the Holy Spirit ourselves, and in those times received intimations of the eternal. We are convinced of the reality of our experience but frustrated by the inability to fully comprehend or to communicate our new insight to others.

Nevertheless, we may be quickened by the Holy Spirit to sense some dimensions of the nature of God and the depths of eternal meanings which go beyond the experience of the temporal environment. As this occurs we say we are quickened by the power of God.

In all of these, however, personal knowledge is so meager that we are subject to great error. The interpretation of those intimations which are received distorts or misses the truth. If we had only these for guidance all would inevitably be lost. We could not grasp the nature of that which is ultimately real and good as contrasted with that which people so often seek, but which in reality has no substance and destroys those who expend their lives and energy for it. For example, history indicates that people have a great disposition to worship idols. These idols eventually take control of the worshipers' lives. People who believe in idols trust them for security, pray to them for success, and offer them sacrifices to cultivate their goodwill. Patterns of life, social relationships, and use of resources may all be determined by belief in an idol which in reality has no power except that which people's faith vests in it. The idol is an unreal god; it exists only in imagination.

The worship of idols is mentioned because this so graphically illustrates the tendency of all people to elevate the imagined to a position of reality while disdaining or ignoring that which is true and substantive. In modern times we have often replaced the graven images of old with technical inventions, scientific knowledge, or wealth. These new images become sources for security and lead us to a vain trust in illusory power which has no ultimate substance.

If humans had been created and then left only to their own devices to learn what is ultimately real, the human race could never have discovered the truth of existence nor found a lasting meaning and purpose for life. Our race would have been condemned to follow the fantasies of its own invention. We would have been like those described by Isaiah:

> Yea, it shall be unto them even as unto a hungry man who dreameth, and behold, he eateth, but he awaketh and his soul is empty; or like unto a thirsty man who dreameth, and behold, he drinketh, but he awaketh, and behold, he is faint, and his soul hath appetite. Yes, even so shall the multitude of all the nations be that fight against mount Zion.—Isaiah 29:8

God Has Sent His Son

As Christians we have faith that God who creates the universe and sustains every part of creation, and who orders the most distant galaxy and causes the tiniest violet to bloom in a meadow, has invested himself in the human race in a most profound way. Because of God's purpose in humanity and his love for all, God has entered into his own creation of time and space as a person. He has become a part of history so that he can identify with people and become the revelation of the true reality of life. God has done this through his Son, Jesus Christ.

In describing the motivation of God to perform such an awesome act, the Apostle John wrote: "For God so loved the world, that he gave his Only Begotten Son, that whosoever believeth on him should not perish; but have everlasting life" (John 3:16).

In describing this amazing thing which God has done because of his love, John said:

He was born, not of blood, nor of the will of the flesh, nor of the will of man, but of God. And the same word was made flesh, and dwelt among us, and we beheld his glory, the glory as of the Only Begotten of the Father, full of grace and truth.—John 1:13, 14

This event, this act in the midst of history, was and is for Christians the birth, life, death, resurrection, and continuing presence of Jesus Christ. It is the good news that God's Son lived as a human being in order to identify with all humanity. Jesus leads us into the truth that we did not know and could never have learned on our own. Christ empowers us and shows us God in time and space concepts that we can understand. This event staggers the mind. Even those closest to Jesus had difficulty comprehending. We are reminded of Philip's lack of comprehension, "Lord, show us the Father, and it sufficeth us." To that request Jesus responded:

Have I been so long time with you, and yet hast thou not known me, Philip? He that hath seen me hath seen the Father; and how sayest thou then, Show us the Father?

Believest thou not that I am in the Father, and the Father in me? The words that I speak unto you I speak not of myself; but the Father that dwelleth in me, he doeth the works.

Believe me that I am in the Father, and the Father in me; or else believe me for the very works' sake.—John 14:9-11

In thinking of the problem which we as creatures of time and space have in comprehending the eternal, we are aware that on our own we are lost; we have no hope. Only as God participates in his own creation, can he disclose the purpose, meaning, and nature of the eternal. The truth of eternity is an essential truth which governs and gives purpose to human existence.

As unfathomable as it may seem, it is our faith that God has entered into his universe through the person of his Only Begotten Son to save humankind. In John's account, Jesus said of himself, "I am the way, the truth, and the life: no man cometh unto the Father, but by me" (John 14:6). And further, "This is life eternal, that they might know thee the only true God, and Jesus Christ, whom thou hast sent" (John 17:3).

To speak of Christ as truth does not mean that one could, through the study of Christ, become an electrical engineer or a medical doctor. Rather, it means that Christ is that integrating truth which brings the temporal and eternal together and expresses the unity, purpose, and value of human experience. The truth revealed in God's presence in history gives meaning and direction to all the temporal knowledge which may be attained through a rational intellectual search. The temporal and eternal are not in opposition to each other but supportive. In a sense, that is the reason why the church through the years has felt that students involved in academic study were helped by an environment of Christian faith and values.

When we think of the significance of God entering into the world through his Son, we affirm that this is the most important event in history. This overwhelming act of God leaves us awestruck.

In Conclusion

By faith we affirm that the universe of time and space is created and sustained by God. Since God is the creator, he is greater than the creation. Therefore, we cannot fully comprehend God because, for the most part, we can only comprehend concepts which we have experienced in our temporal universe.

At the most we have only hints and fragmented thoughts about God and the eternal. It is not wrong to phrase ideas of God in time and space language, but we should understand that language and ideas are feeble attempts to express concepts that are beyond anything people have experienced or known. Even attempts to express personal limitations are inadequate because they must be framed in temporal terms.

In the midst of the human predicament God entered into history using the universe of time and space to reveal in tangible terms the truth about the nature of God, the nature of the universe, human nature, and the way of life which is in harmony with his truth. God has accomplished this by entering into the midst of life as his Only Begotten Son, Jesus Christ, who is himself the way, the truth, and the life. Christ is the "word made flesh"—the eternal expressed in ways we can comprehend.

STUDY HELPS

1. Why is it so difficult to talk about those things which mean the most to you? Recall an experience in which you have had this difficulty. Turn to a class member and share your experience. What is the relationship between a lack of words and a lack of understanding? How are they similar? Different? With your partner, share other situations where this problem exists.
2. What human limitations prevent you from seeing something as timeless and spaceless?
3. What is meant when poeple say they have been "quickened by the power of God"? When have you felt this power? Share an experience with a friend.
4. What is the meaning of the statement found in John 1:13, "He was born, not of blood, nor of the will of the flesh, nor of the will of man, but of God"? How does this scripture fit with an understanding of Jesus as a flesh and blood human being? How was Jesus both human and divine?
5. Why was it necessary that God be born into history as Jesus rather than simply arriving as a mature adult, superperson, or object?

6. What is your understandings about pre-Christian people's access to God's love in light of the statement credited to Jesus, "I am the way, the truth, and the life: no man cometh unto the Father, but by me" (John 14:6)?
7. Write a brief statement of your belief about God and then share it with a partner.
   How is your belief similar to your partner's? Different? For what reasons might these differences occur?

CHAPTER

GOD IS IN CHRIST

The title for this chapter originates in that powerful truth which grasped the early Christians. They sensed that a wondrous act of God had taken place in their midst. Couching this faith in a letter to the Corinthians, Paul wrote, "God is in Christ, reconciling the world unto himself" (II Corinthians 5:19).

This scripture implies not only the reconciliation of people who become reconciled to each other but also the reconciliation of persons to nonhuman creation. Symbolically, this is reflected in the seal of the church and in the scriptures. The book of Isaiah states the following:

> The wolf also shall dwell with the lamb, and the leopard shall lie down with the kid; and the calf and the young lion and the fatling together; and a little child shall lead them. And the cow and the bear shall feed; their young ones shall lie down together; and the lion shall eat straw like the ox. And the sucking child shall play on the hole of the asp, and the weaned child shall put his hand on the cockatrice' den.
>
> They shall not hurt nor destroy in all my holy mountain; for the earth shall be full of the knowledge of the Lord, as the waters cover the sea.—Isaiah 11:6-9

Some people expect the literal fulfillment of such scripture. Others see these statements as evidence that God is in the creative process, bringing harmony and synthesis to all creation; therefore, God in his own way brings peace to the universe. Unfortunately, the human race has been one of the greatest causes of disruption and conflict in the world. This is evident both in conflict between persons and in the greedy attitude of people toward the environment. Resources have been callously snatched from the earth without regard to the fact that they are God's sacred creations.

Part of the work of Christ was to help the world's people sense the sacredness of all things. In this frame of reference we can say that the universe is sacramental; there are no mundane or unsacred parts to it. Persons are called to be responsible stewards who nurture creation. They are not conquerors who have a right to exploit God's handiwork.

This truth is one that has persistently eluded people. Today the environmentalists call us back to the stark reality that human existence may well depend on this recognition of creation's sacredness. The attitude of stewardship is an essential element of humanity's survival.

Christ Is God's Only Begotten Son

Christians declare that God entered dramatically into creation to bring about a reconciliation between humanity and the Creator. God has done this through Christ, his Only Begotten Son.

When Abinadi was permitted to speak to his unbelieving tormentors he said:

> I would that you should understand that God himself shall come down among the children of men and shall redeem his people. And because he dwells in flesh, he shall be called the Son of God; and having subjected the flesh to the will of the Father, being the Father and the Son—the Father because he was conceived by the power of God, and the Son because of the flesh; thus becoming the Father and Son—they are one God, the very eternal Father of heaven and of earth.
>
> Thus the flesh becoming subject to the Spirit, or the Son to the Father, being one God, suffers temptation, and yields not to the temptation, but suffers himself to be mocked, and scourged, and cast out, and disowned by his people. And after all this, and after working many mighty miracles among the children of men, he shall

be led, even as Isaiah said, as a sheep before the shearer is dumb, so he opened not his mouth; even so he shall be led, crucified and slain, the flesh becoming subject even to death, the will of the Son being swallowed up in the will of the Father.—Mosiah 8:28-34

The scriptures express concisely the belief that God has entered into the world to become a part of his own temporal creation. He has always and does continue to reveal himself in the universe in terms that we can comprehend.

God, who is more than or beyond time and space, is not limited to time and space. We must admit that we do not know about the nature of God except as God himself has revealed it. The clearest and most understandable revelation is in Jesus Christ. In Christ, God is revealed in person. In Christ we experience God as the direct confrontation of divine personhood with us as persons.

When dealing with the mystery of God revealing himself in the flesh or in the temporal world as the Only Begotten Son of the Father, we sense a deep and unfathomable unity of Son and Father as one. Christians experience God as the Father and Christ as the Son. The Holy Spirit also is known as God. Persons may actually exclaim after a deeply spiritual experience, "God was with me!"

This is to say that although we cannot fathom or comprehend the eternal God when he enters into the temporal world as one of us, we can comprehend those elements which are revealed in time and space.

We believe God entered into the world in Jesus Christ. When the author of Matthew was describing to the Jews how the scriptures were fulfilled in Christ's birth, he quoted Isaiah, saying, "Behold, a virgin shall be with child, and shall bring forth a son, and they shall call his name Emmanuel, (which, being interpreted, is, God with us)" (Matthew 2:6).

This interpretation of the meaning of the name Emmanuel is in harmony with the earlier quotation, "God is in Christ." This is not to say that being in Christ meant God was no place else. Rather it says that we see in Christ the divine being in the flesh, accepting the limitations of human temporality in order that the revelation can be understood and shared by all.

The symbol of this truth is found in the term "Only Begotten Son." This helps us understand who and what Christ is. As humans we have limited creative power. A carpenter may create a chair, a cook may create a pie, or a musician may create a hymn. *Create* in this sense means to construct from existing materials. When creating any of these things, we know that they are of an order lower than we are. They are subject to us and unequal to us. We never create anything which is of a higher order of existence or greater than we are.

When children are begotten, however, they are of the same order as their parents. When speaking of Christ as being the Only Begotten Son of God, we affirm with confidence that he is not something less than God; indeed Jesus is God in the flesh. To say that Jesus is God in the flesh is to say that God has entered into the temporal world and subjected himself to the limitations and circumstances in which we live. Out of his love for people, God chose to be one of the most lowly among humankind in order that he could reveal the truth people could never have comprehended in any other way.

Paul, writing to the Philippians, said:

> Let this mind be in you, which was also in Christ Jesus; who, being in the form of God, thought it not robbery to be equal with God; but made himself of no reputation, and took upon him the form of a servant, and was made in the likeness of men; and being found in fashion as a man, he humbled himself, and became obedient unto death, even the death of the cross. Wherefore God also hath highly

exalted him, and given him a name which is above every name.—Philippians 2:5-9

There Is Unity in the Divine

As Christians we are not polytheists. We affirm the faith that God is one. In the midst of other polytheistic tribes and nations, the Hebrews proclaimed, "Hear, O Israel; The Lord our God is one Lord" (Deuteronomy 6:4).

This affirmation does not claim that God is in one location or one body, or that God gives attention to only one thing at a time. God is not limited to oneness in that sense, for he hears the prayers of millions of people scattered all around the globe who lift their hearts in prayer at the same moment. While God is listening, he guides the astronaut circling the globe, orders the planets, is mindful of a sparrow's fall, and clothes the lilies of the field.

When speaking of oneness we are saying there is a unity in all our contacts with God. Although we experience God in different ways, we are all experiencing one God.

No temporal illustration can adequately explain this concept of the unity of God. All illustrations distort as well as open one's understanding. Nevertheless, it may be helpful to observe that one of our most common temporal experiences is with water, H_2O. We may experience it as a liquid that fills the oceans or the glass of water on a table, or as hard, frozen ice. We may experience H_2O as humidity that penetrates dresser drawers or forms clouds above the earth. Yet there is a unity about H_2O: it is water in whatever form it takes.

Since we have affirmed that our understanding of God is limited to our experience with him in the temporal world, the significant question is not "What is God like?" We have seen that humanity cannot comprehend that in this temporal life. The significant question is, "How do we experience God?" Christians have traditionally said: We experience God as the heavenly Father, who is the creator and sustainer of the universe. God is the Only Begotten Son, who is God in the flesh, for he has become a part of our history. We have experienced God as the Holy Spirit who is the spiritual presence of God entering into us both individually and corporately in such a powerful and intimate way that he becomes closer than any living human; indeed he becomes part of us, guiding, comforting, judging, strengthening, and revealing the truth to us. Jesus said, "The Holy Ghost beareth record of the Father and me; and the Father giveth the Holy Ghost to the children of men because of me" (III Nephi 13:23).

Because Christian people sense the same divine person so powerfully in all three of these ways, they speak of "God the Father," "God the Son," and "God the Holy Spirit." This is affirmed in such common hymn phrases as "Praise, praise the Father, praise the Son, praise the Spirit Three in One," or the phrase "To God the Father, God the Son, and God the Spirit, Three in One."

This common experience in which we have been confronted by the Father, Son, and Holy Spirit has led us to speak of these as the Divine Trinity. Sometimes Christians have used the term *Godhead.* In the Colossian letter Christ is referred to in this way, "For in him dwelleth all the fullness of the Godhead bodily" (Colossians 2:9). This expresses the faith of Jesus' followers that he was indeed God in a physical body or, in other words, in the flesh.

The exact way of envisioning God varies greatly among people. Certainly God can and does reveal himself in many forms. Realizing that God is eternal and has dimensions beyond the knowledge or experience of any human causes us to remain humble and tolerant of others' beliefs about God. One person's beliefs may be as valid as another's. The Christian experience through the centuries, however, has led us as Christ's followers to speak of Father, Son, and Holy Spirit as the common contact we have with the divine. We also affirm that these are not three different Gods. Such a belief would be polytheism. We can say, therefore, that whatever may be our conception of Deity, we believe in an essential unity of the divine mind and power that created and governs the universe.

In Conclusion

The concept of the Only Begotten Son is the clearest way of saying that Christ is not less than God but is divine. Jesus is God in the flesh. The larger question regarding what God is like always escapes us because we are limited to the temporal world of time and space. God is not limited. We are finite and God is infinite.

We shall not argue about God's characteristics, but rather affirm that whatever God is, we experience him in a temporal world as Father, Son, and Holy Spirit.

STUDY HELPS

1. What is the meaning of the RLDS church seal in light of the comments of Isaiah 11:6-9, quoted on page 21? How may this be a symbolic or literal expectation for church members?
2. The *Funk and Wagnells Standard College Dictionary* defines the word *reconciler* as a person who brings back friendship after estrangement. Consider the role of reconciler in the search for peace. How is the theological understanding of this word different from the more casual usage?
3. Are today's environmentalists just now bringing

humanity to a realization of the sacred nature of the world? How is stewardship a meaningful concept in dealing with the human exploitation of resources?

4. Do you feel that you can know God? Why or why not? Why is it impossible to know God in his entirety? What are ways in which this knowledge is communicated?
5. Consider the meaning of revelation in the author's affirmation: "The clearest and most understandable revelation is in Jesus Christ. In Christ, God is revealed in person." What does this suggest about the value of persons?
6. What is the significance in understanding Christ as God's "Only Begotten Son"? What does the word *begotten* mean? Why is this word important? Write your explanation of the Trinity—Father, Son, and Holy Ghost. Share your belief with another class member.
7. Christians are not polytheistic. What would it mean to your consideration of Christ if a separation between God and Christ was affirmed? Some cultures are polytheistic—for example, Japanese. How would you explain monotheism to people living in these settings?
8. The author discusses the three traditional images of God as Father, Son, and Holy Ghost. With which of these images are you most comfortable? Least comfortable? Why? What other images are meaningful to you? Why? What images would you use to write your statement of belief in God?

CHAPTER

THE CHRIST OF HISTORY

One of the perplexing problems that concern all people is determining when and how something is known. How do we know what we believe we know and how can we test it for validity? Many of us have heard someone vehemently declare that they know "God is" or "This is the true church"—only to find a few years later that the person no longer believes in God or is not active in the church. Couples who on their wedding day sincerely pledge their undying love for each other may at a later date declare that they do not love each other. For some of us there have been times when we have been sure we knew a certain thing only to find later that we no longer know or believe what once seemed so true.

The study of how people know what they know is called epistemology and merits a depth of consideration far beyond the scope of this book. There are elements of this subject, however, that are quite important to the Christian faith. When we say that we believe in God who is eternal and in Jesus Christ his Only Begotten Son, we must of necessity ask ourselves honestly, "How do we know that? What evidence leads to that conclusion?"

There are people who do not share our beliefs about God or Christ. They find meaning for their lives and an explanation for the universe in some other faith. Even Christian people who believe in God and in Christ do not agree in their understanding of specific elements of this faith. That has been a factor in the development of many Christian denominations. It is evident that the bases upon which people arrive at knowing differ one from another.

Ways People Gain Knowledge

If we do not have a way of knowing or do not want to make the effort to know for ourselves, we often accept the explanation of an authority. We may believe something because the scriptures appear to confirm its truth. We go to a medical doctor because we believe the doctor is an authority who can tell what causes our ill health. In the modern world the idea that a truth has been validated scientifically gives it authority. Many say, "It has been scientifically proved that . . ." Such authority is often accepted as the primary source of truth.

Some rely on "a priori" (self-evident or presupposed) experience for arriving at beliefs which are drawn from self-evident conclusions. For instance, most believe that a ball thrown skyward will come back to earth and that fish live in water. In a similar way we may develop other beliefs about values of life which experience has made plain to us.

Most humans find a compelling urge to conceptualize a pattern of belief which they have reasoned out. This is especially true if it completes a meaningful system. We often say, after fitting a belief into such a closed system, that the idea "seemed so right" or "it was so plain"; it seems to fit into our belief system as our hand fits into a well-worn glove.

Much of what people accept as true is passed on from generation to generation. We may accept something because it is commonly believed by society and is a kind of extension of our own experience as we learn from the experience of others. In this way we avoid the mistakes others have made and are enriched by their successes.

Some persons depend on mental and spiritual illumination as the source of knowledge. This may be called the "inner light." Many religions rely heavily—some almost exclusively—on the inner experience. This is sometimes encouraged and cultivated by prayer, fasting, and meditation. Some people use a drug such as peyote as a part of worship because they believe it stimulates mental receptivity. Some stimulate an inner experience through meditation or the chanting of certain phrases which are intended to shut out the environment and lift the worshiper's focus so that he or she becomes oblivious to physical hungers, drives, and passions. This often leads to an asceticism in which the worshiper practices strict self-denial as a way to spiritual achievement. The result is a dualism in which the physical universe is considered to be in opposition to the spiritual. Other people may base their beliefs on extrasensory perception, mental telepathy, inspiration, or even intuition.

The value of inner experience is well known and reflects those characteristics which are uniquely personal. When people rely on inner experience as the source of knowledge, however, they often find it is subject to great error. The inner experience is perceptual. It is always an amalgamation of the thought patterns and past beliefs of the individual, the spiritual illumination which has quickened the mind, and the reflective process which presses these into a meaningful system of beliefs. It lacks any objective means of validation and therefore is not easily tested.

Since each of us has a different system of belief and reflective processes, we find ourselves accepting an idea that others may not accept because it does not fit their mental construct. Conflicts arise, along with the question, "How do you know that?"

It becomes evident that the inner, reflective experience is subject to error. When we follow our own systems we may be convinced that a certain thing is true because it fits our system of belief, but upon testing the idea, it may be shown to be in error.

While religion has been especially subject to the inaccuracies caused by dependence on the inner light, other methods of knowing the truth are subject to error also. We have no totally reliable way of knowing what is true. We probably do best when considering the evidence from all valid sources rather than basing our belief on only part of the available evidence.

A Comprehensive Christian Faith

One of the strengths of the Christian faith is that it does not reject any source of truth. Based on both objective historical experience and the inner revelatory illumination, its truth is validated in a priori experience as well as logic.

When Joseph Smith was in doubt about the religious claims of his day, he was guided by the scripture which states: "If any of you lack wisdom, let him ask of God, that giveth to all men liberally, and upbraideth not; and it shall be given him" (James 1:5). Joseph's experience as he responded to the scriptural direction was confirmation of the inner light. Through this Spirit he received prophetic powers.

We tend to emphasize the inner experience when relying on prophetic guidance for direction and light today. We often speak of this illumination of the mind and soul as the indwelling of the Holy Spirit.

In the Christian system of belief, however, we do not rely alone on inner light or illumination. We value the inner experience, but must test it against the objective experience of other persons and of history. Even a message extrapolated from an experience of divine illumination must be tested against the experience of history, especially as it is recorded in scripture.

For Christians the objective experience of God's action in history is equally important to the inner light. Throughout the centuries, God has objectively revealed his truth. This truth has been preserved in the Hebrew and Christian culture and communities, in history and in scriptures. The scriptures are, in a sense, the memory of the church about its experience with God throughout the centuries. There are few greater guarantees for keeping the church free from apostasy than a keen knowledge of the scriptures and a sensitivity to the spirit and attitude expressed in them. The church is, however, always open to new revelation which is always to some degree disjunctive with the past. We therefore need to be careful not to so immerse ourselves in interpretations of past scriptures that God is unable to break into our present history with genuinely new revelation.

We are constantly confronted by the equally valid sources of knowing found in the truths revealed in the objective experiences of history and the subjective experiences of inner light. As these are pressed against each other, they show distortions of belief which can then be corrected.

For the Christian the universe is not dualistic. The physical world is no less a part of God's creation than the spiritual. We perceive the truth most accurately when we remain open to God's truth and will as it is revealed in both objective and spiritual realities.

There are no absolute proofs to validate assumptions about ultimate reality. We assume the existence of a God and that there is purpose and meaning in human existence, not because of absolute proof but rather because such assumptions about the nature of existence are most in harmony with all the experience and knowledge we have gained. Augmenting this are the beliefs that have been passed on from history and other people.

If our judgments of truth are to be most accurate, we need to open ourselves to the evidence which comes from all sources. Unfortunately, when knowledge begins to disagree with beliefs already held, we sometimes condemn the source and refuse to consider the evidence. The Christian can never afford to do this. Faith must be examined in light of all the evidence available. Unexamined faith is always weak. As the common weight of evidence supports our faith, we have greater assurance of its truth.

In considering, testing, and living by the faith we have accepted, we may come to say, "I know this is true." When making such an assertion, we mean that we have validated this idea or belief by our own experience and under circumstances so compelling as to make contradiction unthinkable.

How Do We Know Jesus Is the Christ?

This concern about knowing is a very important element in commitment to Christ. Christians believe Jesus is the Only Begotten Son of God. The Jews, however, believe that Jesus is not the Christ but was rather a great rabbi, a wise teacher, a good man. Many other non-Christian people do not accept Jesus as Emmanuel, meaning "God with us."

Scholars have tried to discover records or other evidence bearing on the life of Jesus. Generally, their search among secular sources has been in vain. Scholars and theologians have come from the search saying that Christian sources of information are so fragmentary, uncertain, and full of polemical doctrinal biases that very little can be ascertained historically about the life of Jesus.

Jesus was born of common parents. It is not likely that anyone in his own time would have kept a record of his existence or actions. No attention was given to the boyhood or even the ministry of Jesus in secular history. And although the gospels later recorded that the events attending his birth and death were miraculous, the masses of people were unaware of them at the time.

Our Source Is the Scriptures

We do have scriptural accounts which contain the testimonies of some who knew Jesus personally. These "eyewitness accounts" were passed on orally and recorded later by others. Scripture also includes the writings of people who were a part of the early church and were close to the historical events that marked the ministry of Jesus. The biblical authors' purpose for writing was to convince and convert rather than to record history. Details of the life of Jesus depicted in the New Testament scriptures are not always reliable. However, the fact of his existence, ministry, and impact on early followers can hardly be denied or ignored. The scriptures through the centuries, when thoughtfully and honestly evaluated, have provided a source of testimony about the birth, life, ministry, and death of Jesus. These have sustained the realities of Jesus' historical existence. For Christians the testimony of the scriptures also includes affirmation of the resurrection, final ministry, and ascension of Jesus. This testimony is not only supported by the scriptures but also by the continuing testimony of the church which exists to witness good news to the world.

The Christ of Faith

In more recent years, some scholars who have searched secular history for the record of Jesus' life have said that the evidence for Jesus' existence is so meager that he is most appropriately accepted as the "Christ of Faith." By this they mean that the nature of Jesus' actual existence is unimportant; the important thing is the faith of the people which, when lived out, has proved true. It is this lived-out faith, they say, which has sustained Christians for nearly two thousand years. The significance of Christ for these persons is not so much in the history of his past as in the assurance of his spiritual presence and in the hope which this gives for the future.

We would certainly not want to argue against this kind of faith. The Apostle Paul was forthright in declaring the witness of the Spirit as an essential element of belief. He said:

> Wherefore I give you to understand, that no man speaking by the Spirit of God calleth Jesus accursed; and that no man can say that Jesus is the Lord, but by the Holy Ghost.—I Corinthians 12:3

For most Christians, however, the reality of Jesus as a historical person is so great that it cannot be ignored. The overemphasis of one element of faith so that it is pulled out of perspective is the stuff from which most heresies are made. We affirm, therefore, that much of the strength of Christian theology and faith is its basis in recorded account, subjective reflection, and spiritual illumination. While Christians have sometimes fallen short in their willingness to be open, the basis of our faith leads us to believe that God, who creates all things, expects us to be ready to receive the truth from every source of his creation. God gave humanity both a tangible historical revelation and a spiritual revelation in his Only Begotten Son, Jesus Christ.

In Conclusion

All people search for some integrating faith that gives meaning and purpose to their lives and explains and justifies their institutions and social structure. Much of that faith is transmitted as a part of the process of growing up in a particular culture. Like the sons of Helaman who said, "We do not doubt our mothers knew" (Alma 26:57), we all in some fashion absorb much of our faith from those we trust. Inasmuch as we rationally accept our faith, however, we assume as true those beliefs which seem most in harmony with all of our experience.

A strength of the Christian faith is its basis in historical and objective elements, the logic of systematic construction, and illumination of spiritual powers which link us with the eternal. The greatest safety in "knowing" is that the knowledge we accept as true is tested and based on broadly examined sources and comprehensive evidence. God expects no less.

STUDY HELPS

1. Describe how you go about making a decision. How does the pattern of your decision making serve as a good model to aid in understanding your beliefs? What procedure do you follow for determining your beliefs? What is the source (authority) of your belief?
2. What comes first, belief in God or faith in God? Do you consider belief the basis of knowledge or does belief arrive after having knowledge? How did you arrive at your position?
3. What is meant by "common sense"? How is this a productive way to know something? How does people's own history affect their ways of knowing? What sources of knowledge are apparent in the belief in common consent?
4. In small groups list at least six events in the life of Jesus. Then share these with the class and make a combined list of events. In what way do scriptural references differ from more secular records? Why

has such an important event generated so little documented evidence from other, even unfriendly, witnesses?

5. Describe to the class your response to the suggestion that belief in Christ as the Only Begotten Son is blind faith? What is the nature of blind faith?

   What are the characteristics of faith that is not blind?
6. Some scholars have suggested that a rational faith is impossible. In light of the author's views, how is a rational faith possible? Why is it not a paradox?
7. Write a brief statement describing your faith in Jesus Christ. How has your faith helped you? In what ways has it grown and changed over the years?
8. The author refers to "inner experience." What do you think he means? Identify any of your own inner experiences. How important is this kind of experience to your faith?
9. What do you think the author means by "objective historical experience"? How does one identify, evaluate, and share such experience? Identify such experiences in your own life. How important are they to your faith?
10. Discuss with others in the class the relative importance of inner and objective experiences in your determination of truth and belief.

CHAPTER

THE CHRISTIAN STUMBLING BLOCK

Religions are primarily concerned with explaining the ulimate reality of existence. This involves such matters as creation, the nature of the universe, human origins, the social structures of society, the ultimate purpose of existence, and the meaning of life. Religions may develop a system of belief which explains these matters and answers the persistent human questions about why the universe is as it is and what humanity's purpose and role is. At that point they have a vested interest in protecting and promoting that explanation. Religions as a result often resist new information because it may change the conception of the universe which was previously explained. Such changing views may cast doubt on the validity and reliability of the faith.

Good examples of this struggle are seen in the way the sixteenth-century church opposed Copernicus and later Galileo as these scientists advanced such theories as the daily rotation of the earth on its axis and the revolution of the planets around the sun. Far from being pleased that greater knowledge had been discovered, the church tried to keep these theories from reaching the public. People did not want the new viewpoint because they felt threatened; it challenged their beliefs about the nature of the universe and eventually even their beliefs about themselves.

In such situations religious leaders may try to conserve the past and oppose new developments which disturb past concepts. When cast in this role religious leaders become obstacles to progress.

This was the circumstance which confronted early Christians. Jesus was accused by the Jews as being dangerous because, they said, "He stirreth up the people, teaching throughout all Jewry, beginning from Galilee, to this place" (Luke 23:5). The problem, however, was not alone the teachings of Jesus, but that Jesus became identified as the Son of God.

God's human intrusion into the world was such a profound act in history that it forced new ways of looking at life and its purpose. This new faith could not be accommodated in the old social and religious structures. Jesus had indicated this fact to the Pharisees:

> For when that which is new is come, the old is ready to be put away. For no man putteth a piece of new cloth on an old garment; for that which is put in to fill it up, taketh from the garment, and the rent is made worse. Neither do men put new wine into old bottles; else the bottles break, and the wine runneth out, and the bottles perish; but they put new wine into new bottles, and both are preserved.—Matthew 9:21-23

The old and the new do not blend together because they are not compatible.

It was this incredible new way of looking at life that eventually caused the people to reject and persecute Jesus and his followers. They wanted to rid themselves of what seemed to be a threatening new heresy. Saul, in his early life, was one of the leaders in this attempt to exterminate the new faith. He understood the opposition well. He wrote this thoughtful comment after his conversion:

> For the Jews require a sign, and the Greeks seek after wisdom; but we preach Christ crucified, unto the Jews a stumbling block, and unto the Greeks foolishness; but unto them who believe, both Jews and Greeks, Christ the power of God, and the wisdom of God.—I Corinthians 1:22-24

The Christian Uniqueness

One of the problems people had in grasping the idea of God's presence in the world was its uniqueness. Some have called it the "particularity" of the Christ event.

As humans we generally try to organize our knowledge of the world and understand things in light of the fact that they fit into a classification which we can relate to our whole environment. Jesus, however, defies such classification. He is not one of a class of Christs. Only naïve Christians try to make Jesus' birth, death, and resurrection more believable by showing that someone else did something similar. Jesus is unique. In him God acted in the world in a way that is not, as far as we know, ever to be repeated. Our faith, therefore, is not subject to repeated experiments which can be tested for accuracy. Because of the uniqueness of the Christ event it is a "stumbling block" or "foolishness" to many people in every generation.

The Expectations of the Jews

As a Messiah and deliverer of the Jews, Jesus fell short of meeting their expectations. Their nation had been humiliated and trampled under the feet of conquerors for centuries. They were expecting a Messiah from the lineage of David, but they expected such a one to become a national hero by conquering their enemies and making the nation a world power.

Throughout the Old Testament is the assertion that God would bring victory to his people and make the nation great as a means of showing the superiority of his power over the gods of foreign tribes and kingdoms. For the Jews of Jesus' time, their achievement of political power and freedom was not merely a desired benefit for them; it was also an important step in the witness that the God of Israel was the only true God.

They therefore expected the Messiah to be a leader

who would free the nation and "redeem Israel" (Luke 24:20). On those occasions when Jesus had performed miracles which indicated his great and unusual power, the people had immediately interpreted this to mean that he was the strong and mighty one whom God had raised up to be their king (John 6:15). A savior would save the nation and the people, but by so doing he would also show that Jehovah was really God.

The prophet Isaiah had said:

> For unto us a child is born, unto us a son is given; and the government shall be upon his shoulder; and his name shall be called Wonderful, Counselor, The mighty God, The everlasting Father, The Prince of Peace. Of the increase of his government and peace there is no end, upon the throne of David, and upon his kingdom, to order it, and to establish it with judgment and with justice from henceforth even for ever. The zeal of the Lord of hosts will perform this.—Isaiah 9:6, 7

It is not surprising then that the Jews were expecting a Messiah who would be a divinely endowed world leader. They expected him to redress the wrongs which had been heaped on them, to punish the wrongdoers, and to establish the nation in the prestigious position which they felt it deserved.

Jesus was not such a man. The Jews did not find in Jesus the evidences they expected in the Messiah. To them he was an imposter who assumed a role which was nothing short of blasphemy. The humble, unmilitaristic nature of Jesus and his unwillingness to be a political leader were stumbling blocks for the Jews.

Christ's Understanding of Himself

Interesting matters of conjecture through the centuries have been the questions, "How did Jesus grow to understand his mission?" and "When did Jesus perceive himself as the Messiah?"

When God entered into the temporal world as a person in Jesus, he gave up or emptied himself of those

Godlike advantages that could have made him different from humanity. Because of God's willingess to do this, we declare that Christ was "wholly man" as well as "wholly God." This is to say that Jesus Christ, the Only Begotten Son of God, chose for our sake to divest himself of any characteristics not shared by us so that we could see in him what it is possible for us to achieve. When speaking of Christ as being "wholly man" and also "wholly God," we are not implying that he is two different individuals in one. Rather we say that united in one person is that being who is God and who is also the perfect human person. Jesus is the man who lives out the eternal in the midst of humanity. These are not two separate things; they are one. We hint at this when speaking of atonement as at-one-ment with God.

While all illustrations fall short, it might be helpful in understanding the unity of the divine and the human in one being to point out that a woman may be considered by her husband to be the perfect wife and the perfect mother, but she is one woman.

While the scriptures do not clearly declare when or how Jesus came to know that he was indeed the Christ, we must conclude that this knowledge and the implications of being God's Only Begotten Son were a growing and developing comprehension.

Whatever else may be involved in Jesus' understanding of his own identity, it appears that in a major way he came to see his mission with its staggering implications at the time of his baptism. The experience itself, accompanied by the divine confirmation of his Sonship, rested on him with such weight that he went into the solitude of the wilderness where he spent forty days in fasting and preparation to enter into his work. The dangers of focusing Jesus' ministry on unworthy objectives were caught up in the temptations which came to him as he emerged. It appears that he sensed from that time on a great urgency of divine purpose and calling.

The Dawning of Human Recognition

After Christ's ascension the disciples recognized that his whole life had been marked by evidences that he was the Messiah. The events surrounding his baptism and ministry had pointed to his identity as the Christ, but in a sense the historical Jesus became the Christ for humanity at the point where other persons became aware that Jesus was the Christ.

This then is the glorious but unfathomable mystery. Jesus, the man, is Christ, the divine Son of God. When he is referred to as "Jesus Christ" or "Jesus who is the Christ," that name is the essential affirmation of the Christian faith. When speaking of the historical Jesus, we call into focus that facet of his being which is declared when we speak the name Jesus.

The eventual Christian testimony grew out of those experiences in which others recognized Jesus as the Christ. Christianity was born, not so much with the birth of the baby Jesus as in that crucial moment when Peter affirmed, "Thou art the Christ, the Son of the living God" (Matthew 16:17). The Christian faith was born then and will continue as long as there are persons who meaningfully repeat that confession. God's intrusion into history is not complete with Jesus' own recognition that he is the Son of God. That knowledge must be shared by other people. Jesus puts the question to the human race: "Whom say ye that I am?" (Matthew 16:16). The intrusion of God into the world must be recognized by persons who are the object of his love.

Jesus rejoiced greatly when Peter sensed his identity and mission. However, in the same moment that the disciples recognized him as the Christ, the earthly powers of humanity rejected him. Jesus could not be the Son of

God without recognizing that the Christ would die as the price of accepting that title. Those very disciples who continued to grow in their knowledge that Jesus was the Christ were unknowingly affirming the paradox that the Christ who confronts the estranged world as its Savior must participate in the self-destructive results of human estrangement. The atonement and reconciliation were not extended to humankind from an alien source but from One who identified with the human race. The road from the estranged person to the redeemed person passes through the awesome abyss of the crucified Christ.

Perhaps the beginning step on the Christian road is the understanding and interpretation of the affirmation, "Jesus is the Christ."

The Calling of the Church

Christianity and the Christian faith are dependent on the continuing knowledge of Jesus' earthly life and ministry and the declaration that he indeed is the "Christ, the Son of the living God." The sobering meaning of this concept is that the church or fellowship of persons in the world who have received the testimony that Jesus is the Christ is the crucial link on which the future of the divine act of salvation rests. If it should happen that the knowledge and historical tradition emerging out of Jesus Christ's advent on earth were lost completely, we would have lost the effective meaning and value of that which God has done on earth by sending his Only Begotten Son. Christ is not only Christ for today because he is God's Son but also because he is *recognized* as God's Son. Tradition says Peter was the first to affirm the fact in his statement, "Thou art the Christ, the Son of the living God." If this is true it was in that moment that Christianity was born. It is in that continuing revelation that the church is sustained.

Today the possibility of total catastrophe is no longer unthinkable. The stories of the flood or of the Nephite people were once considered casually, as incidents in which great destruction came to humankind, but as past accounts far removed from today. Now they are reminders that indeed it is possible for such destruction to occur, leaving no memory of the Christ event. If that should happen no single person could affirm that "Jesus is the Christ." The destructive powers used in modern warfare make this possibility vivid to all.

We confront the future in faith that God directs the affairs of history in such a way that his work is preserved and his kingdom achieved. Yet such a statement reflects a faith by which disciples live, not a guarantee supported by history.

If the continuation of the Christ event rests on the Christian church, its crucial responsibility to witness that "Jesus is the Christ, the Son of the living God" is a most holy and primary responsibility. The church must proclaim the Christ of history to the world. When the church is vague about this responsibility or is drawn aside to become a promoter of ethics, economic well-being, charismatic exulation, its own self-aggrandizement, or any other goal which diminishes its effectiveness in the witness that "Jesus is the Christ" and the meaning of that affirmation, it has to that degree fallen short of its mission.

The temptation for many to think of such shortcomings as apostasy is justified, but this must not be treated as a black-and-white issue. As humans, we always fall short of our high calling as disciples of the Lord Jesus Christ. Nevertheless, we also know that God's patient, loving influence has never ceased to be experienced, especially in the fellowship of the church. History reveals certain times when the degree of apostasy was greater and more widespread than at others. It has been said that "the light burned low," but since the testimony of the Christ event has continued in the fellowship of his disciples from the days of his earthly ministry until now, we must affirm that the authority of that testimony has never been lost. It is part of our faith that the testimony will never be lost. We have been privileged to be called into Christ's church in this generation to continue the declaration.

The Stumbling Block

The Christian affirmation that Jesus is the Christ has been the stumbling block to many who have heard the gospel since the days when Jesus walked the roads of Judea. Many can accept Jesus as a great teacher, a good man, a wise and sacrificial philosopher, but they find the unique Christian declaration that Jesus is the Christ, the Son of the living God, beyond belief. In a sense it is always beyond human comprehension. At this point divine intervention intersects with human faith. This is in harmony with the response of Jesus to Peter's first confession that Jesus is the Christ: "Flesh and blood hath not revealed this unto thee, but my Father who is in heaven" (Matthew 16:18).

The church is called to witness, but that witness must always be carried on the wings of the Holy Spirit if it is to enable others to surmount the stumbling block of unbelief.

In Conclusion

The Christian witness was and is a stumbling block to the world because it discloses a unique act of God in the world. Jesus Christ can never be explained as an example of a category of christs. His advent cannot be repeated for scientific observation.

For us, Jesus becomes the Christ when we recognize him as God's Son. The witness of his divinity is experienced through the testimony of the Saints and the power of the Holy Spirit. To proclaim that witness and to bring the power of Christ to bear in the lives of people is the chief calling of the church. The testimony that Jesus is Christ may be a stumbling block to the skeptic, but it is the power of salvation to those who believe.

STUDY HELPS

1. Read Matthew 9:21-23. How does this passage relate to the church's concept of an open canon? How does this scripture reflect on the call for openness to change?
2. Why was the idea of Christ's uniqueness such a problem for the Jews? How does this problem relate to previous discussions concerning how people know things?
3. Why was it necessary for Jesus to be "wholly man" as well as the Son of God? Many believe in the principle of like kind. Experience indicates that Hispanics witness naturally to Hispanics. How does this relate to the idea that people learn from other people?
4. What is the relationship between atonement and reconciliation? Look up the words in a dictionary. What is the difference or similarity between them?
5. What does the author mean by the "awesome abyss of the crucified Christ"? How have you experienced this realization?
6. What is your definition of apostasy? The author views apostasy in a fairly broad manner, page 46. Where do you see apostasy in this sense present in the church today?

   In what ways is this the nature of the church? How

does the church deal with the problem of apostasy?

7. *Exploring the Faith* (Herald House, 1970), page 129, notes that

   > apostasy is ever present with us. Just as Paul cautioned against the "grievous wolves" that would not spare the flock and rebuked the teachers of the Galatian saints who perverted the gospel of Christ, so we need to recognize the fact that every generation has its wolves and perversions. Because of the sin within us, we are constantly in danger of bending the gospel to serve our own purposes rather than God's. We tend to use the power and structure of the church to serve our selfish ends.

   How might people bend the gospel to serve their own purposes? How is this statement similar to or different from the author's view?

8. What do you think is the probability that a catastrophe will occur that could block out all memory of the Christ event? If this happens, what future would there be for Christianity? How might God choose to reveal himself in the face of such a catastrophe? How has God revealed himself in remote areas where Christianity was unknown for centuries?

9. What stumbling blocks stand in the way of persons accepting Christ in today's world?

CHAPTER

JESUS, THE MAN FOR ALL

A major concern to the early Christian church was the confusion in the minds of Christians about how Christ could be both human and divine. While Christians in more recent years have struggled with such questions as the virgin birth and the resurrection in an attempt to show the divinity of Christ, members of the early Christian church struggled with questions about whether or not he was actually human. They questioned whether or not he was physically born and grew to adulthood, experiencing the same growth, temptation, pain, and limitations experienced by other humans. The early church had less trouble believing that Christ was divine than that Christ was really human.

The Docetic Heresy

One of the earliest Christian heresies was Docetism. This was the belief that Christ only seemed to have a human body; therefore, he did not really suffer pain or death on the cross as humans suffer pain and death. For the Docetists there was no doubt that Christ was divine, but they argued that being of the divine order, in reality he only appeared to be physically human and only appeared to experience the limitations and frailties suffered by humanity. In a similar manner Docetists reasoned that persons who were born of the Spirit lived on a different level from that of the physical world. Therefore, after their conversion and spiritual rebirth, it made little difference what they did in the physical world. The spiritual and physical were only remotely related to each other.

This problem has not ceased to exist. The Christian faith has found it necessary to insist on the humanity of Jesus Christ. Many people wanting to glorify Christ have in one way or another tried to deny his full humanity. In their zeal to protect what they believe to be the true Christian faith, they emphasize the deity of Christ in such a way that Jesus was not really a person at all.

We See Ourselves in Jesus

Perhaps one of the greatest dangers in Docetic reasoning is that it easily leads to the conclusion that Jesus could be the perfect person because he was not subject to the same sufferings, weaknesses, temptations, and limitations that we humans experience. Therefore, he is not an example to us because we can never attain to his divine stature. Unfortunately some persons have pressed the idea of the superhumanness or deity of Christ to refute the use of his standard of life as a judgment on human frailty. After all, if Christ was divine, how can humans be expected to attain Christ's standards?

The error in this belief begins to be clear when we discover that Christ cannot be our savior if he was of a different order and therefore not subject to the same conditions of life experienced by us. While the early creeds and confessions of faith of the church affirmed the divinity of Christ, they emphasized equally his humanity. He was, they said, "perfect God and perfect man" in one Christ.

This is in harmony with the Hebrew letter in which it is said of Christ:

> Forasmuch then as the children are partakers of flesh and blood, he also himself likewise took part of the same;. . . For verily, he took

not on him the likeness of angels; but he took on him the seed of Abraham. Wherefore in all things it behooved him to be made like unto his brethren,. . . For in that he himself hath suffered being tempted, he is able to succor them that are tempted.—Hebrews 2:14, 16-18

Jesus Grew Like Other Humans

The belief in Jesus' humanity is clearly present in the scriptures. Matthew and Luke depict Jesus' body being formed in the womb of a human mother and born as a helpless baby. He is described as gradually growing to adulthood. The following is found in the Doctrine and Covenants:

> And I, John, saw that he received not of the fullness at the first, but received grace for grace; and he received not of the fullness at first, but continued from grace to grace, until he received a fullness; and thus he was called the Son of God, because he received not of the fullness at the first.
>
> And I, John, bare record, and lo, the heavens were opened and the Holy Ghost descended upon him in the form of a dove, and sat upon him, and there came a voice out of heaven saying, This is my beloved Son.
>
> And I, John, bare record that he received a fullness of the glory of the Father; and he received all power, both in heaven and on earth; and the glory of the Father was with him, for he dwelt in him.—Doctrine and Covenants 90:2

The implication here is that Jesus achieved an important level of understanding and spiritual power when he committed himself in baptism. It was perhaps then that he began to understand the implications of his messiahship.

Luke states, "And Jesus increased in wisdom and stature, and in favor with God and man" (Luke 2:52). Here Jesus has been described as growing in four categories. First, he grew physically and chronologically. He developed from a baby into a mature adult. There was nothing unusual about this physical maturation. Second, he grew in wisdom. At birth Jesus, as far as we know, was a normal baby. He had the mind of a baby. It too developed as he grew and learned. Jesus was, therefore, a child of limited knowledge and wisdom. He lived in Nazareth as the carpenter's son for approximately thirty years and neighbors did not think of him as unusual. Third, he grew in favor with God. The account implies that God's confidence and delight in Jesus' youthful character increased as he successfully met ever harder and more exacting tests. Fourth, Jesus grew in favor with other people but they all thought of him as the carpenter's son.

> And when he was come into his own country, he taught them in their synagogues, insomuch that they were astonished, and said, Whence hath this Jesus this wisdom and these mighty works? Is not this the carpenter's son? Is not his mother called Mary? And his brethren, James, and Joses, and Simon, and Judas? And his sisters, are they not all with us? Whence then hath this man all these things? And they were offended at him.—Matthew 13:55-57

They were offended because they were sensing that one who was a common person among them was exercising power and authority over them.

Jesus showed hunger for knowledge at the age of twelve when he was in the temple with the leading teachers. Even though "all who heard him were astonished at his understanding, and answers" (Luke 2:47), there is no suggestion that he was anything other than fully human. Jesus returned to Nazareth and, far from assuming a position as a superhuman teacher, was obedient to his parents.

Jesus Experienced Fatigue, Hunger, and Pain

The scriptures report that as an adult Jesus grew weary. He became hungry and thirsty. He slept. He sorrowed for the death of a friend. He was lonely and greatly dreaded the experience of his own torture and death at the hands of his persecutors.

Although Jesus was "Emmanuel (which, being interpreted, is, God with us)" (Matthew 2:6), for our salvation God was born and lived among us sharing all the limitations and circumstances of life. Jesus was not protected or given some power unavailable to others. He was, as the scripture assures, "made like unto his brethren" (Hebrews 2:17). Isaiah prophesied of him, saying:

> He is despised and rejected of men; a man of sorrows, and acquainted with grief; and we hid as it were our faces from him; he was despised, and we esteemed him not. Surely he hath borne our griefs, and carried our sorrows; yet we did esteem him stricken, smitten of God, and afflicted.—Isaiah 53:3, 4

Jesus Identified with Humanity

It was not because God is limited that Christ came among humans as a person. This was God's way of communicating with his human creation. He participated with persons in their lives. John said of him, "And the same word was made flesh, and dwelt among us, and we beheld his glory, the glory as of the Only Begotten of the Father, full of grace and truth" (John 1:14). He became identified with humanity. Because of his love for people, the great God and Creator of all became humbled and took on himself the limitations of his own human creation, even to suffering a physical death, that he might genuinely live out in our midst the life available to all. The statement in the scriptures, "God so loved the world, that he gave his Only Begotten Son, that whosoever believeth on him should not perish; but have everlasting life" (John 3:16), is affirmation of an awesome act of God and a price paid by divine love which staggers all imagination.

Jesus Experienced Temptation

One of the significant elements of Jesus' humanness was his vulnerability to temptation. He was subject to the same temptations which beset people. Three of the Gospels relate accounts of Jesus being tempted in the wilderness soon after his baptism. These temptations were focused on personal desire for food in a time of great hunger, for a spectacular but shallow means of achieving success, and for earthly power. They were all genuinely human but they also involved temptations often experienced by leaders. Such temptations lure leaders away from the difficult course of persuading persons to righteousness and holiness by love. This course of action is much harder than buying their allegiance with gifts of things or captivating them through works of magic or compelling their obedience through power and force. The church has consistently contended with these temptations—to expand the church by use of economic help and welfare, by dazzling people with miraculous power, and by making the church an attractive and powerful body with which to be associated.

The statement, "When the devil had ended all the temptation, he departed from him for a season" (Luke 4:12), indicates that Jesus experienced other temptations later. They drove him to his knees in the Garden of Gethsemane and must have lurked even in the shadow of the cross. The fact that in his humanness he faced the temptations victoriously gives us hope that we too can achieve victory. We can affirm our hope with the writer of the Hebrew letter: "For we have not a high priest which cannot be touched with the feeling of our infirmities; but was on all points tempted like as we are, yet without sin" (Hebrews 4:15).

Jesus Was the Great High Priest

From the scriptural record it appears that the growth of Jesus included an increasing awareness of his divine calling and an unusual motivation to be true to his purpose and role as the Son of God. Clearly he was not insulated from the circumstances of life which beset the human race.

In the Hebrew letter Jesus is spoken of as "a great high priest" (Hebrews 4:14). The nature and function of the high-priestly work is also described:

> For every high priest taken from among men is ordained for men in things pertaining to God, that he may offer both gifts and sacrifices for sins; who can have compassion on the ignorant, and on them that are out of the way; for that he himself also is compassed with infirmity. And by reason hereof he ought, as for the people, so also for himself to offer for sins.—Hebrews 5:1-3

Just as Jesus served among the people—sharing their circumstances, bearing his own burdens as well as theirs, offering up sacrifices, petitioning God for himself as well as for them, and driven by compassion for people because he shared their weaknesses—so every high priest is called to function. The glory is that God takes the weakness of the committed, repentant, struggling person and uses it to save his people.

Jesus Was Obedient

Jesus not only experienced human frailties but also had to subordinate himself to God as do other people. On numerous occasions the scriptures testify of his prayer and supplication to God. Sometimes he asked for direction as when he selected his twelve apostles or for personal strength as when he prayed in Gethsemane. Sometimes he prayed for his disciples and the work he had established. In Gethsemane he yielded his struggling will to the will of his Father as he prayed, "Nevertheless, not my will, but thine be done" (Mark 14:40). While in this hour he achieved victory over his own fear and dread, he was yet to cry out from the cross, "My God, my God, why hast thou forsaken me?" (Mark 15:39).

In John's record Jesus says, "The Son can do nothing of himself, but what he seeth the Father do" (John 5:19), and, "For I can of mine own self do nothing; because I seek not mine own will, but the will of the Father who hath sent me" (John 5:31).

In Conclusion

God entered into the world and into history through his Son, Jesus Christ. Jesus also evidenced human limitations. He became subordinate to the Father to live out in very truth the life which all of us live in the circumstances which are common to humanity. The uniting of God's holiness and perfection with humanity's weakness and limitation has always been a mystery. The awesomeness of this act, the condescension of the mighty Creator, the love of the heavenly Father, and the mystery of his redemption can never be plumbed by the finite mind. If we could comprehend the infinite purpose and nature of God we would be equal with him. Since this can never be, we must always fall short; but it is that great chasm between the finite personhood of humankind and the infinite majesty, holiness, and power of God that is bridged by faith in the depths of worship at the feet of Jesus Christ.

We do not comprehend in full, but know God to be dependable and have integrity. We trust our lives to him fully, confident that he is able and willing to save us for his purposes.

STUDY HELPS

1. What is Docetism? Why is it considered a heresy? How may this be a contemporary problem?

2. How do you relate the perfect nature of Jesus Christ to his experience of human suffering, fears, even shame? Can Jesus comprehend, for example, the nature of divorce, having never made the kind of commitment persons make in a marriage? Why or why not? How does your answer reflect how you know God?
3. Humans are inclined to slip over the growing-up days of Jesus and concentrate on his public ministry. What might Jesus' life have been like as a young child? A teenager? A young man in a Jewish world? What does this tell about the Christ of history?
4. The temptations of Christ suggest that he was touched with life's burdens. Identify the temptations of your life and think how Christ might have responded. How would his responses be the same as yours? Different? Discuss your temptations with another class member. Then share what you envision to be Christ's reaction to your specific concerns. Then do the same with your partner.
5. You or another student may like to read chapter 2 of *Exploring the Faith* (Herald House, 1970) and share a summary of it. How does this statement help you understand what the author is saying? What about it is clearer, more explicit, helpful?
6. Of what significance is the reference to Jesus as the great high priest? How might his ministry be compared to that of other priesthood offices? How is the ministry of Jesus comparable to the ministry to which all Christians are called?
7. How can Jesus' obedience to God serve as a model for the obedience of disciples today? In what ways can you be obedient to God's call?

CHAPTER

JESUS, THE TEACHER AND LEADER

Religion has always been a primary interest of people, but the strategic location of the lands at the eastern end of the Mediterranean made this area a hotbed for the generation and growth of religious concepts. Because of its location it was a place where people from the civilized nations of Africa, the Middle East, and Europe met in trade and travel. Jerusalem and its environs was a key crossroad. Caravans traveling from Egypt to Assyria or Babylon would most likely pass through the land of Judea. Commerce between Greece or Rome and the Middle East was probably by water to a port on the eastern Mediterranean and then overland to the Middle Eastern nations involved. This mixing of the people of many civilizations at the crossroads of travel and commerce led to the active ferment of ideas.

The cross-fertilization of ideas was further heightened by wars and military conquests in the area. Located between Egypt and the nations of the Middle East, Judea was often right in the path of military conflicts. The country frequently sought friendship and protection through alliances with larger nations, and in so doing was influenced by their systems and cultures. All too frequently Judea was conquered, resulting in domination by foreign countries. It was precisely this kind of foreign cultural imposition that led to the Maccabean Wars and the rise of the Pharisees as a group dedicated to keeping the Jewish faith free from alien heresies.

The religious faith of the people was an ever-present concern of the prophets. It is seen all through Old Testament scriptures. The Hebrew people were severely scolded for worshiping foreign gods and following the religious practices of neighboring nations.

The World of Jesus

Jesus was born into this country in which religious controversy was common and religious alternatives found everywhere. Judea was under the domination of the Roman Empire when Jesus was born. People's minds were exposed to ideas about the nature of the universe and religion, sin, divine rewards and punishments, and a host of explanations for the world in which they lived.

The ministry of Christ did not begin in an empty world but in one already filled with religious belief. Jesus was able to build on that which had already been taught. As a result, much of his life apparently was lived in preparation for his active ministry. As far as is known, his formal education did not extend beyond the synagogue school. This was normal for the youth of his community. He was nonetheless a learned teacher. Multitudes followed him because he taught the words of life with a simplicity and power they had not before experienced (Matthew 8:1).

After Christ's baptism he entered into his ministry interspersing it with fasting, prayer, and periods of solitude. In a three-year period he revealed the depth of his preparation and his keen observation. His most striking illustrations were taken from his knowledge of the written word and from commonly observed incidents in everyday life.

It has been said of our time that just when we gained the technical power to beam a message around the world we found we did not have a message. Such an appraisal could not be made of Jesus. Those who heard "were astonished at his doctrine; for he taught them as one that had authority, and not as the scribes" (Mark 1:20).

The Authority of Jesus

The word *authority* has many facets. One of these emerges from its Latin roots. The Latin word *augere* means to create or produce; the English word *author* has its origins in this word. Hence, as Jesus built on the established concepts of the people, he authored new religious concepts which pierced the minds of his hearers with such clarity and force that multitudes were drawn to listen. There was no repetition of stale platitudes in his message; his words and ideas came with fresh insights. They answered the yearning of many hearts. His words and his actions were like sparkling fountains in contrast to the dry legal arguments of the learned scribes and Pharisees.

Jesus was the author of the doctrine which challenged the legalism of his contemporaries. When the Pharisees challenged Jesus because his hungry disciples plucked and ate corn on the Sabbath, the book of Mark records the following response:

> The Sabbath was made for man, and not man for the Sabbath. Wherefore the Sabbath was given unto man for a day of rest; and also that man should glorify God, and not that man should not eat; for the Son of Man made the Sabbath day, therefore the Son of Man is Lord also of the Sabbath.—Mark 2:25-27

The scribes and Pharisees brought to him a woman who had been taken in adultery, saying:

> Now Moses in the law commanded us, that such should be stoned; but what sayest thou? This they said, tempting him, that they might have to accuse him. But Jesus stooped down, and with his finger wrote on the ground, as though he heard them not. So when they continued asking him, he lifted up himself, and said unto them, He that is without sin among you, let him first cast a stone at her. And again he stooped down, and wrote on the ground. And they which

heard it, being convicted by their own conscience, went out one by one.—John 8:5-9

While these examples illustrate the principle by which Jesus brought fresh insights to the law, they are only two of many such confrontations with the legalism of his day.

Master of the Paradox

Jesus was bold enough to dare to use paradox as a teaching method. The use of the paradox shook people out of their lethargy and made them think. Jesus was not tamely consistent in his speech. He said, "He who seeketh to save his life shall lose it; and he who loseth his life for my sake shall find it" (Matthew 10:34). John testifies that Jesus said to the woman who came to draw water from a well, "If thou knewest the gift of God, and who it is that saith to thee, Give me to drink, thou wouldest have asked of him, and he would have given thee living water" (John 4:12). Jesus was willing to risk the misunderstanding of "consistent" minds to send forth the deeper truth that was hidden by the mental shackles of persons.

Inclusive Authority

As a teacher Jesus was open to all in need. He was not puritanical in any false sense. Righteousness and holiness emanated from his life and those who were touched by him were changed. Nevertheless, he was willing to challenge custom and associate with the ungodly and disinherited. When he was criticized for such association he said, "They that are whole need not a physician; but they that are sick. I came not to call the righteous, but sinners to repentance" (Luke 5:31, 32). His disciples included persons whose lives had been remade by their association with him, but they came from varying backgrounds. One was a hated tax collector, another a disgraced woman, and several were common fishermen. He was a person for all.

The Authority of Knowledge

In the use of the word *authority*, we often imply knowledge, insight, or skill. Scholars have authority regarding the subjects they have studied. This authority of competence was recognized in Jesus' day. For example, the rabbi was an adult of authority because he was a learned man.

The competence and learning of Jesus were marks of his authority. Although his teachings were often couched in paradox, offensive to the self-righteous, and incompatible with the old religious structures, they carried the authority of competence. They were often inconsistent with traditional practices and beliefs.

Jesus acknowledged the incompatability of his doctrine with the traditional:

> For when that which is new is come, the old is ready to be put away. For no man putteth a piece of new cloth on an old garment; for that which is put in to fill it up, taketh from the garment, and the rent is made worse. Neither do men put new wine into old bottles; else the bottles break, and the wine runneth out, and the bottles perish.—Matthew 9:21-23

Nevertheless there was such a sense of rightness about his teachings that those who heard could not remain uncommitted. They felt the truth in their hearts and minds. They either welcomed his message or turned against him when they sensed what this truth would do to their social structures and religious beliefs. They recognized, however, that here was the authority of competence. If Jesus had not been so "right," they would have dismissed him as one more radical misfit who did not deserve their attention. It was because they recognized that he must be taken seriously that many opposed him.

Authorized by God

Jesus also carried the power of conferred authority. Persons may have authority conferred on them, as when they are elected or appointed to office. Jesus made it clear that as a human he did not have certain powers; he acted by the power conferred upon him by God who is the center of all authority, "For I can of mine own self do nothing; because I seek not mine own will, but the will of the Father who sent me" (John 5:31). Because Jesus' teachings were of this authority he said, "Although the days will come that heaven and earth shall pass away, yet my word shall not pass away; but all shall be fulfilled" (Matthew 24:36).

The authority conferred on Jesus led men and women to seek him out for learning, healing, comfort, and counsel. With Nicodemus, many could say, "Rabbi, we know that thou art a teacher come from God" (John 3:2).

Jesus' Methods of Teaching

Many have suggested that Jesus was a master teacher because of the effectiveness of his teaching methods. While he taught as one having authority, he also used devices for teaching which helped people understand. He used such teaching devices as the parable which put concepts of deep spiritual and social significance into commonly understood terms. He used nearby tangible objects to teach spiritual truths. He referred to the lilies of the field to illustrate God's dependable care and took a little child in his arms to help persons understand the openness, humility, teachableness, and faith of God's children. The people he healed, the feasts he attended, and the death of a close friend provided occasions for him to teach vital and compelling lessons.

Eventually the meaning of all Jesus' ministry came to focus in that last week. The lessons of the Last Supper, the trial, the crucifixion, and the resurrection are unsurpassed as the carriers of the gospel Jesus came to teach. In a more accurate sense, Jesus did not come to *teach* the gospel as much as he came to *be* the gospel. Perhaps this is why he is known as the "Great Teacher." He is the gospel message. In everything he taught, Jesus revealed the potential within persons to become the sons and daughters of God.

The Effective Teacher

In the long run the effectiveness of a teacher is determined by the way the teacher influences the students. In this sense Jesus taught people effectively. His followers had diverse styles of life. They were poor and rich, sick and healthy, despised and popular, and often they had sinned grievously. Jesus was the one who brought them a new sense of worth. He healed, encouraged, brought hope and repentance, and gave a new strength to the lives he touched.

People whose lives were transformed by Jesus could not describe what had happened to them any better than to say they had been "born again" or had become new persons in Christ. Those who observed were also aware that the lives of the followers of Jesus had been wondrously changed. When Peter and John went out in ministry after Christ's ascension, the scriptures describe the people's reaction as follows: "Now when they saw the boldness of Peter and John, and perceived that they were unlearned and ignorant men, they marvelled; and they took knowledge of them, that they had been with Jesus" (Acts 4:13). The effectiveness of Jesus as a teacher is validated by the Christian movement and the fact that every generation looks to the gospel for direction, hope, and comfort. He is the master teacher of all time.

Jesus' Command to Teach

Jesus was not only the great teacher himself. A high

priority on the teaching responsibility of his followers is contained in the scriptural charge to the Twelve, "Go ye therefore, and teach all nations,. . . teaching them to observe all things whatsoever I have commanded you" (Matthew 28:18, 19). The teaching of Jesus is extended in his followers in every generation and in his church. To be effective Jesus' teaching must be incorporated into the lives of those who teach so that it is expressed in all that they are as well as in what they say. Jesus' charge to the Twelve concluded with the assurance that he would be with them "always, unto the end of the world" (Matthew 28:19). His Spirit helps persons become the gospel, and his Spirit wings the message with authority into the hearts of those who learn.

Not in Word Only

In the years after the ascension of Jesus the band of followers often rehearsed the experiences they had shared with Jesus. It seemed to them, however, that the instruction which he had given in so many ways while he walked and dined and lived with them was constantly being renewed and updated in the fledgling church. Before he left them he had promised to send the Comforter who would abide with them forever: "The Comforter, which is the Holy Ghost, whom the Father will send in my name, he shall teach you all things, and bring all things to your remembrance, whatsoever I have said unto you" (John 14:26). Although Jesus was gone, it seemed to the disciples that he was still present, still in their minds and hearts, teaching and blessing them.

It is inadequate to say that Christ *was* a great teacher. He continues to teach through the Holy Spirit. This does not mean that the Holy Spirit goes beyond the revelation in Christ, but rather that the meaning of the revelation brought in Jesus is constantly being expanded and deepened as the Holy Spirit brings to memory his life and opens meanings not previously grasped. This was so evident in the early Christian church that Paul, in writing to the Thessalonian saints, said, "For our gospel came not unto you in word only, but also in power, and in the Holy Ghost, and in much assurance" (I Thessalonians 1:5).

In Conclusion

Jesus is a great teacher. Most of us seldom comprehend the depths of what it means to be such a person. Jesus is not a great teacher merely because of the wise and good things he said but because of the total person he was. He is the "Word made flesh." He is the teacher to lead beyond all other teachers.

STUDY HELPS

1. If possible, obtain *A History of the Christian Church* by Williston Walker (Charles Scribners Sons, 1959), and read chapters 1 and 2 in period 1. You or another class member may like to share the historical events at the time of Jesus' birth. What was happening in the Roman Empire and Jewish situation? What is the significance of Jesus being born into a world of religious activity and controversy? How did these events shape the life, ministry, and death of Jesus?
2. Why do you think that Jesus spoke in paradoxes so often? What is the nature of paradox? Look up the word *paradox* in a dictionary and see exactly what it means.
3. In considering the nature of authority it might be helpful to read pages 8-17 of F. H. Edwards' *Author-*

ity and Spiritual Power (Herald House, 1956). Share your findings with the class. What is Edwards' definition of authority?

4. What was the nature of Jesus' education? How did his knowledge relate to his authority? How did he practice the things he learned?
5. In education, learning occurs when the students assimilate knowledge, understand its implications, and apply its ramifications to their lives. Relate these three points to the experience of Zaccheus as recorded in Luke 19:1-10. What did he learn at a conceptual level? Exploration level? Life application level? When have these three steps occurred in your life?
6. Why is Jesus assumed to be such a great teacher? Make a list of what you think is necessary for someone to be a great teacher. How is teaching more a matter of example than it is the transference of knowledge?
7. Review chapters 9 and 10 in Elton Trueblood's *Confronting Christ* (Harper, 1960). What does Trueblood say concerning the responsibility of the listener? Share this with others in class.
8. Discuss the nature of Jesus' parables. What is it about parables that enable them to be such powerful bearers of the gospel message?
9. Discuss the author's assertion, "Jesus did not come to *teach* the gospel as much as he came to *be* the gospel." How can you most effectively *be* the gospel?

CHAPTER 7

CHRIST, THE HEALER

The Christian gospel is centered in life. When thinking of the ministry of Jesus, we inevitably remember his healing the sick and even raising the dead. Jesus is the Lord of life. When teaching his disciples he said, "The thief cometh not, but for to steal, and to kill, and to destroy; I am come that they might have life, and that they might have it more abundantly" (John 10:10).

Life and health have to do with living. They are positive and because their source is God, Christians acknowledge that life is sacred—a divine gift. Beliefs about the sacredness of life vary. Some non-Christian religious groups consider the taking of any life repugnant; they will not kill an animal. Other religions hold the belief that only people of their own faith, race, or tribe are sacred.

Those who understand and believe the Christian faith accept the principle that God is the creator of the universe. Because this is basic to our faith, we recognize that everything is sacred and believe in a sacamental universe. God is at work, fulfilling his own purposes in creation.

Persons are called as moral beings who comprehend in some degree the divine purpose: to share with God in the nurture of the universe. Their calling is to participate intentionally with God in the fulfillment of his purposes. As they do this they share with God in bringing health and wholeness to creation. The Saints have referred to this responsibility as stewardship.

There are, of course, God-given laws which function to maintain the health of the divine creation within the frame of our limited and finite existence. These are sometimes referred to as the laws which maintain the balance of nature. Some environmentalists believe that human intrusion into the environment generally disrupts nature's laws. The human ambition to conquer, harness, exploit, and consequently to pollute is the enemy of the natural environment. In a sense, people make creation sick and destroy the health of the world; in so doing they eventually destroy themselves. This is to say that human life and health are directly tied to the health of all the world.

When persons view the world in this light they cannot remain idle in the belief that the laws of nature will automatically fulfill God's intent, nor can they by their own greed exploit and destroy. Rather they are called as stewards to learn to understand God's creation as far as human intellect can perceive and to actively share in the nurture and cultivation of the natural world.

Jesus Recognized the Sacredness of Creation

Jesus lived in the temporal world and recognized the world's response to God's loving, creative power. This is portrayed almost in an offhand manner in the following teachings:

> Behold the fowls of the air, for they sow not, neither do they reap, nor gather into barns; yet your heavenly Father feedeth them. Are ye not much better than they? How much more will he not feed you? Consider the lilies of the field, how they grow; they toil not, neither do they spin. And yet I say unto you that even Solomon, in all his glory, was not arrayed like one of these.—Matthew 6:29, 32, 33

Jesus often pictured God as the husbandman who pruned and cultivated his orchard. He condemned the unresponsive and the unprofitable.

This is in harmony with the cosmic concerns expressed in the scriptures. While people have been most interested in human values and human redemption they should not overlook the fact that God actively creates and sustains all existence in time and space. This total fulfillment of God's purposes is symbolically indicated by such terms as a "new heaven and a new earth" (Revelation 21:1) and Isaiah's description of the eventual reconciliation of the earth (Isaiah 11:6-9). It is not helpful at this point to interpret prophetic statements about the future, but to indicate only that God's concern includes his total creation. It is important to understand that human health is but a part of the larger work of God.

Jesus Made People Whole

Jesus healed in response to the need for health as wholeness. The term *wholeness* includes the total functioning of the person to fulfill the purposes of God in creation; it is not merely relief from pain or the rebuking of a sickness. This is illustrated in the experience of Jesus with the impotent man at the Pool of Bethesda:

> And Jesus saw him lie, and knew that he had been now a long time afflicted; and he said unto him, Wilt thou be made whole? The impotent man answered him, Sir, I have no man when the water is troubled, to put me into the pool; but while I am coming, another steppeth down before me. Jesus said unto him, Rise, take up thy bed and walk. And immediately the man was made whole, and took up his bed, and walked.—John 5:6-9

The question which Jesus asked focuses the need for healing on a much larger issue than the man's physical condition. The man obviously wanted to be healed of his limiting physical affliction. Rather Jesus asked, "Will you be made whole?" This is the insistent question Jesus puts to everyone. In the narrow sense people want to be healed from crippling sickness, but do they want wholeness? Wholeness implies repentance and reorientation of attitudes, habits, and total life to God's purposes.

How far are people willing to go in abetting the process of being made whole? Are they ready to eliminate the known causes of lung cancer, including cigarettes? Do people want to give up the jealousies, destructive competition, or anxieties which are the source of hypertension?

In the struggle of our estranged existence the sources of ill health are often lodged within us. They involve inner conflict, vagueness of purpose, hatred, self-indulgence, and a host of attitudes toward the self, other people, and God which must be yielded before we can be made whole. Sometimes ill health is caused by acts and habits which are destructive. These often arise out of the human predicament. This does not imply that all sickness is the result of disobedience to God's law. Much of the world's illness is for reasons over which no person has control. Nevertheless, the healing process does involve changes of attitudes and life commitments.

The Apostle Paul was conscious of this when he counseled the Corinthian saints about the way in which they had been observing the Lord's Supper. He said: "For he that eateth and drinketh unworthily, eateth and drinketh condemnation to himself, not discerning the Lord's body. For this cause many are weak and sickly among you, and many sleep" (I Corinthians 11:29, 30). Wholeness is the reorientation of the person to full commitment to God.

Healing Is Intrinsic to the Gospel

When a person has hope, a purpose for loving, reconciliation with the environment including other persons, and the inner peace of an unqualified faith in God, the forces which produce health can function to bring wholeness. Jesus spent much of his ministry in restoring health and wholeness to persons.

When Jesus caused the sick to be healed or the dead to live we attribute the action to his miraculous power. Indeed it is the confirmation of our faith that God is the source of all life. In its larger dimensions, however, the healing ministry of Jesus must not be separated from his total mission. Physical healing was an extension of his role in saving humanity. Physical healing is a part of and interrelated with all the other facets of the ministry of Christ.

The redemptive ministry of Jesus reconciles people to God. It helps realign lives with the ongoing purposes of God. It is the predicament of everyone to be caught in a world of conflicting values, expectations, and human desires. These conflicting forces come both from without and from within. They set persons at odds with themselves, with each other, and with God. For many, the most needed element in restoring health is reorientation. Persons need to be restored to "faith, hope, charity, and love, with an eye single to the glory of God" (Doctrine and Covenants 4:1e). This positive element is the substance of life. Negative elements are destructive. They are in opposition to the creative power of God and associated with darkness, cold, hate, and nonbeing.

Jesus' healing was always associated with faith and hope and light. He calls persons symbolically to walk in the spiritual light of faith. When this happens even death is transformed—from the fear of nonbeing to the joy of rebirth. It is the door to immortality. The health which Jesus brought was therefore not a contradiction of death.

Death Is a Part of Life

Christians who assume that death is a denial of faith, or that it is a failure of God's intent, do a disservice to the gospel. They do not understand the revelation of life symbolized in the resurrection. When God established a temporal world in which all persons die, he did not make some gruesome mistake, nor did he invest death with evil. Rather he helped us understand that death is but a part of life and does not in and of itself change the character of our lives. The evil which has been built into persons' lives and the righteous qualities developed will be intrinsic to what persons are after death as well as before.

Laying On of Hands Is a Healing Ordinance

Saints understand the ordinance of the laying on of hands for the healing of the sick in the light of the wholeness which Jesus brings to persons in the temporal world. This ordinance is intended to bring wholeness to persons who are sick. It should be an experience of worship in which all concerned approach God, the author of life, yielding their lives to him and asking his blessing of health on the one who is ill. The faith and repentant understanding of the elders and those who join in support is required, as well as such willing repentance as the one who is sick can offer to God in the sacrament. When this is done the powers of the Holy Spirit will come in confirmation and in the restoration of wholeness. Persons must understand, however, that such wholeness does not always mean physical healing. Instead there may come a reconciliation to God and his world, the restoration of "an eye single to the glory of God." Persons feel at one with God and ready to yield their lives to his will.

The following is in harmony with this understanding of the ordinance of the laying on of hands for the healing of the sick:

> The elders of the church, two or more, shall be called, and shall pray for, and lay their hands upon them in my name; and if they die, they shall die unto me, and if they live, they shall live unto me.—Doctrine and Covenants 42:12d

The promise is not that all shall be physically restored but that the ministry of the gospel through the ordinance brings reconciling wholeness. This wholeness is effective in life or death, for the ordinance causes people to yield their lives completely to God. Those who come to God in that kind of faith and devotion need not fear rejection.

Again in the same spirit is the statement in James:

> Is any sick among you? let him call for the elders of the church; and let them pray over him, anointing him with oil in the name of the Lord; and the prayer of faith shall save the sick, and the Lord shall raise him up; and if he have committed sins, they shall be forgiven him.—James 5:14, 15

The promise of the scriptures is a ministry of wholeness for both life and death as the Lord wills. The sick are saved and reconciled. Their sins are forgiven, but such reconciliation and forgiveness come only as persons reorient their lives. Through an experience of repentance they yield their lives to divine power.

The Community of Faith Participates

The experience of healing has greater dimensions than the relationship of an individual to God. Persons live in community and are supported and re-created daily by that community in concert with the Divine. The uniting of the community and the eldership in faith to support those who, because of age or the circumstances of illness, are unable of themselves to cope with the situation in faith is recognized as a part of the healing process. Many have witnessed the healing of a baby or an unconscious person. These were blessed by divine power.

The church is that community committed to the purposes of God and empowered to function through the ordinances and sacraments in very specific ways to assist in bringing wholeness and health to humankind.

Sickness May Not Be Evidence of Sin

There are mental and spiritual dimensions which influence health and wholeness in significant ways. The attitudes, purposes, and positive commitments of life are factors in human health which Jesus always addressed in this ministry. We cannot assume, however, that sickness is necessarily the result of sin. Like the visitors to Job in his affliction, persons who have tried to relate the causes of illness to a person's disobedience to God are neither correct in their assumptions nor helpful to the one in distress. On the occasion when Jesus saw a man who had been blind from birth, his disciples questioned him, saying, "Master, who did sin, this man, or his parents, that he was born blind? Jesus answered, "Neither hath this man sinned, nor his parents; but that the works of God should be made manifest in him" (John 9:2, 3).

At first we might assume that Jesus meant God had purposefully caused this man to be born blind so Jesus could heal him and thus demonstrate the divine power of healing. After a more thoughtful consideration of Jesus' comment, however, we become aware that all persons are called to bear whatever circumstances life brings in such a way that the works of God are manifest. Every person carries some burdens and as disciples of Christ we each use the total mix of life to declare the glory of God.

If we allow the negative, self-centered, destructive elements to seep into our lives, health and wholeness are diminished. On the other hand, these very limitations under the guidance of God's Spirit may become the means of great service. All sickness is not caused by sin, disobedience, rebellion, or other negative attitudes or actions; rather sickness is transformed by God into wholeness, both in life and in death, for those who yield their lives to him in response to the ministry of Jesus.

In Conclusion

Jesus is the great healer. He did not merely heal persons nearly two thousand years ago, but his followers through the centuries testify that he has brought wholeness to their lives. His followers do not escape death. Rather life and death have been transformed by Jesus.

Health as brought to humanity by Jesus was not limited to the physical or mental but was a part of his total ministry designed to redeem the race; it was an intrinsic part of the gospel. To believe in God is to believe in the source of life. Jesus brought persons to God who, as the author of life, renewed and redirected them.

Life with Christ ties the present to the future and links human existence with the eternal. "And this is life eternal, that they might know thee the only true God, and Jesus Christ, whom thou hast sent" (John 17:3).

STUDY HELPS

1. What is the relationship between the wholeness of Jesus' healing ministry and current attempts to see the health sciences in terms of wholeness? What is being asked by Jesus when he queries, "Will you be made whole?"
2. The author states that death is a part of life. How does this relate to the wholeness of the person? What is the significance of death if it is not a change in the "character of life"? How may Jesus be speaking of death in a different manner than people generally do?
3. Why may the author assume that the experience of healing is a community, rather than a personal, affair? What does this mean to the ministry of healing for those who stand apart from the church?

What does this impose on congregations as they seek to serve as community? How are the needs being met in your own congregation? What improvements could be made?

4. The author seems to be making two conflicting statements: "In the struggle of our estranged existence the sources of ill health are often lodged within us" (page 72) and "We cannot assume, however, that sickness is necessarily the result of sin" (page 76). How are these contradictory? How can this contradiction be resolved?
5. In the preceding statement it seems possible that some sickness must be the result of sin. How does this relate to the Saints' belief in administration to the sick? When persons ask to be administered to, what is the nature of the healing that can be assured them? What is there other than the love of God that can be asked for in terms of their wholeness?
6. Webster's dictionary defines sick as "affected with disease or ill health; of, relating to, or intended for use in sickness; spiritually or morally unsound or corrupt; sickened by strong emotion; mentally or emotionally unsound or disordered; lacking vigor." How does this meaning compare with that meaning the Saints see in terms of personal belief in Christ's message?

CHAPTER

THE PREDICAMENT OF "THE FALL"

Christians have traditionally believed that "the Fall" is a decisive element in the human predicament. It usually has been related to the Genesis account of the Garden of Eden story. The symbol of the Fall, however, has such universal significance that it cannot be confined to the biblical narrative. The problem represented in this symbol is recognized by most religions. It is the human cry, "Why are we caught in the web of our existence as if we are suspended somewhere between the bondage of earthly selfishness and the freedom of spiritual nobility?" All persons are caught between their dreams of "perfection" and their inability to achieve the vision. Robert Browning in *Andrea del Sarto* wrote, "Ah, but a man's reach should exceed his grasp, or what's a heaven for?" We can contemplate and desire more than we can ever achieve. Individually this is experienced as we fall short of what we know we ought to be and sincerely want to be. Corporately it is experienced, perhaps in its most devastating dimensions, as we struggle to overcome the causes of war.

The Fall therefore is not a story that took place one day in ancient history. It is an ever-present situation, experienced by all people in every age. The question of the Fall is the *why* of estrangement—estrangement from both the earth of human habitation and the God who calls us out of time and space into the eternal.

Many thoughtful persons doubt that the Garden of Eden story ever literally happened. When acceptance of this story and other such narratives is made a test of fellowship in the church, people get bogged down in controversies about the literary vehicle and miss the concept of the Fall as it pertains to the human dilemma.

The role of historical events in the development of the Fall is not the crucial question; rather the fact of the human predicament caught up in the symbol is the concern. This is the question the Christian gospel addresses. When the biblical story is viewed from this perspective the principles set forth are as cogent and up to date as the latest explanation of a modern theologian, anthropologist, or psychoanalyst.

Members of the Reorganized Church of Jesus Christ of Latter Day Saints have traditionally believed all creation, in the spiritual sense, is and was resident in the mind of God. Since we do not have adequate language to express the relationship of our time and space creation to eternity, we generally speak of this as the spiritual creation. In a sense the Fall is a way of describing the transition from the perfection in the mind of God to our estranged existence in this temporal universe.

The Genesis stories can guide the search and provide deep insights into the nature and problems of human estrangement. Modern studies do not replace these insights; they open windows revealing meanings and fresh understanding of the profound revelation already expressed in the biblical account.

The Risk of the Fall

Scriptures point to the fact of human creation as transcending all other things. Persons were created in the image of God. Only those who are created in the image of God have power to rebel and separate themselves from God; therefore, both the greatness and weakness of persons are lodged in the nature of creation.

The potential of the human race for glory could not exist without the risk of humanity becoming satanic. That is the divine risk portrayed by the scriptural story of Satan proposing that humans be created without agency but the Son of God saying, "Father, thy will be done, and the glory be thine for ever" (Genesis 3:3). John could therefore refer to Christ as "the Lamb slain from the foundation of the world" (Revelation 13:8). This was God's fully accepted cost when he created persons in his image and after his likeness. The possibility of the Fall was therefore an inevitable element in the Fall itself.

The Problem of Being Free

The gift of freedom is intrinsic to human creation in the image of God. It is no coincidence that the story of the divine commitment to accept the risk of granting human agency precedes the narrative of the Garden of Eden. The one gives meaning to the other. The risk involved the awesome cost of redemption. The tension between the exercise of human freedom and our destiny to become sons and daughters of God is at the center of the human dilemma. These two poles stretch the souls of persons who are suspended between them.

As compared to other animals, persons have freedom. They possess language and the ability to think and communicate in the abstract. This frees them from the shackles of the concrete situation to which other animals are bound. Persons are free because they have the power to reflect and decide without exterior stimulation. They can penetrate deeper levels of reality and ask questions about the universe, about themselves, and even about God. They are free insofar as they accept moral and spiritual imperatives which open the vision to the eternal. Persons are free because they can plan and play with imaginary structures that are above and beyond anything they have actually experienced. Thus they create worlds above the existing world. They dream what ought to be and then create their visions.

People are also free to negate and contradict their divine natures. They may choose to destroy their own humanity and become the negative influence on others. This is at the heart of sin; it is the satanic power within every accountable person.

The Finitude of Persons

Although we as persons enjoy freedom above all other creatures, our liberty is finite. We feel the call to the infinite freedom of God but fall short of the aspiration. It is as if we are suspended between the bondage of creatures and the infinite freedom of God. Of ourselves we are unable to bridge the gap between our finitude and the hope of the eternal. Caught in this predicament and unable to know what the future holds for us, we become anxious. We know we do not measure up to the holiness of the divine, yet we find it hard to muster faith for that which is beyond our own known power to achieve. Wanting to control our own destiny, we find it difficult voluntarily to release that control to God. We feel restless, estranged, and alone. Understanding this human condition and glimpsing the hope in Christ, Augustine said, in supplication to God in *Confessions*, "Thou hast formed us for Thyself, and our hearts are restless till they find rest in Thee."

Realizing Human Potential

The potential in freedom is awesome and that weight is the human burden. We are liberated from the concrete situation of the environment to soar on the wings of contemplation and frame abstract thought in language which facilitates the idea and communicates it to other people. In exercising this tremendous potential we may dare to imagine structures of society and actions which have never before existed. We may ask questions about ourselves and our relationships with other people and with God. These questions are born out of interests, personal needs, selfishness, and altruism. Such excursions of the mind involve so-called dreaming about the future. Such dreaming causes humans to be aware of unrealized potentials. It precedes the actualization, or real experience. Prior to the time we have become aware of the possibility of a reality we were not free regarding that matter; we are freed when the dream is born. Nevertheless, after the dream brings awareness of the possibility but before we have acted on the thought to bring it into reality, we remain in a state of "contemplative innocence." One may reject an idea and try to force it out of mind or replace it with other thoughts, but the possibility of actualizing the idea is there. One may find the idea good and act upon it. From such dreams the kingdom of God exists in the mind and spirit even though it has not become realized. Out of such contemplation the writer of Hebrews could say of his faithful ancestors:

> These all died in faith, not having received the promises, but having seen them from afar off, and were persuaded of them, and embraced them, and confessed that they were strangers and pilgrims on the earth.—Hebrews 11:13

Contemplation, therefore, anticipates the actualization or rejects the idea, but the basis of that decision is inevitably made by accountable humans in the tension between their understanding of moral law and their desire for the experience. Humans are faced with the crucial question, "Is it right or wrong?" The human predicament, however, makes the actualization of one's thoughts a mixture of rightness and wrongness; it is not a simple decision between that which is clearly right or that which is clearly wrong. Persons may work in jobs that they feel are not fulfilling their life's stewardship, but their jobs seem a required means for supporting their families. People are involved in the military defense of a nation but have apprehensions about the morality of war. Persons make decisions about marriage and divorce when the rightness and the wrongness of the issues are not clear, but decisions must be made. The imperatives of rightness make actualization necessary, but the anxiety and guilt resulting from what is perceived to be wrong inevitably haunt the person.

When the contemplation is actualized the state of innocence is lost. In its place there are the knowledge, power, and joy, or the disappointment of experience. There are also the accompanying anxiety and guilt when the action is seen, either in total or in part, as wrong or when there is uncertainty as to the resulting consequences.

Dealing with Temptation

The possibility of the transition from contemplation to actualization is experienced by persons as temptation. Because the actualization of one's dreams so often is accompanied by some degree of negative results and guilt, temptation is used to denote the desire to actualize that which is wrong. The concept of many Christian people is that the actualization of the sex experience is in fact the primary negative element involved in the Fall. Sex is a universal drive leading to a major source of dreaming and temptations which begin early in the life of persons. Yet it is but one of the many elements involved in the experience of the Fall. The sexual elements are not the cause of the Fall nor its central core but one of the easily identified and universal ways in which the consequences of the Fall may be experienced.

Innocence is not perfection. Before reaching the age of accountability children develop many habits and ways of acting which are wrong. Because of immaturity they are innocent until they reach the state of awareness that the action has moral significance. Children in immaturity are not perfect, but insofar as they lack awareness of right and wrong they are innocent. Whatever one believes about the development of the human race, that state which existed prior to the Fall was a state of innocence characteristic of those who have not developed a sense of moral consciousness. This is symbolized by the partaking of the fruit of the tree of the knowledge of good and evil. This may be seen as the evolutionary development of moral consciousness in the human race or the maturing growth of each person.

The human predicament is that persons are always caught between maintaining the innocence of a potential which has been opened to them by contemplation without losing that innocence through actualizing the experience. The experience is mixed with the knowledge, power, and anxiety which accompany it. Persons recognizing this characteristic sometimes wistfully wish for the innocence of childhood, but children must grow up. They cannot avoid the consequences of the Fall.

Becoming Self-aware

The transition from innocence to actualization is complicated by the innate desire of persons to be superior to and have dominion over all else. While we generally do not understand this characteristic in ourselves, our disposition is to challenge and destroy or conquer anything which is a barrier to our achievement or casts a doubt about our superiority. We are impelled by our anxieties and strive to guarantee the future for ourselves. We dream our own paradise and imagine we are strong enough, wise enough, and good enough to achieve our own salvation. Symbolically this is illustrated in the story of those who tried to build the Tower of Babylon. Most of us are offended by people or things that imply that we are not as good or as capable as they. As we become adult we often do not ask questions because we feel that the questions would reveal our ignorance or weakness. Eventually persons may even challenge God by rebelling against him and taking his name in vain. This is a way of showing their disdain for God; in so doing they feel elevated above or acceptable to other people.

The efforts of people to save themselves and become superior lead them to exploit each other and the environment. In the attempt to elevate themselves at the expense of the remainder of God's creation, people become satanic. Their struggle is destructive, unfulfilling, and illusory. They also destroy themselves in the process. This is perhaps but an expression of the scripture which notes that "the wages of sin is death" (Romans 6:23). People acquire idols to help them achieve their aspirations because they can control the idols. Accepting God as the author of salvation requires personal surrender and "fallen persons" rebel against that. This is at the heart of the concept of "original sin." An innate vanity makes people think they can save themselves and therefore they are unwilling to yield their lives to God.

The Book of Genesis

Best estimates indicate that the written manuscript of Genesis did not come into being until about 400 B.C. Genesis was not one of the first of the Old Testament books. In the period of history in which it was written writers selected and compiled the stories, explanations, and history which had been passed down in traditions. The material selected was that which had the most meaning for the people at the time it was compiled.

The early stories in the book of Genesis were those which gave meaning to people's ultimate questions of creation, their understanding of God, their own nature and purpose as persons, and the origins of their relationship, institutions, and patterns of life.

The Adam and Eve Story

The Adam and Eve story focuses on the explanations and understandings people had about themselves at the time the stories were compiled. The ancients' concern was, "How did people come to be as they are?" When viewed from this perspective, the stories set forth with amazing clarity and astuteness their faith regarding the Fall.

The story begins with the divine intention to create in the human race the power to exercise agency, which is the finite freedom to choose. This freedom is essential to enable persons to become sons and daughters of God, or in other words, to be in God's "image" after his "likeness." The power which seeks to take away that characteristic or gift is the satanic power even when it parades under the guise of saving people. Such satanic power is condemned. The divine commitment to create persons with the freedom of agency included God's fully understood intention to bear the unfathomable cost of human creation.

The story portrays Adam and Eve in their state of innocence exercising their powers of freedom. They were tempted to actualize the possibilities opened by those powers. The consequence was knowledge through which they were confronted by moral consciousness. This moral awareness is represented by the partaking of the tree of the knowledge of good and evil. While the scripture tells of a symbolic evil power urging Eve to eat the fruit of the tree, Eve is also portrayed as eager to eat when the possibilities were suggested to her mind:

When the woman saw that the tree was good for food, and that it became pleasant to the eyes, and a tree to be desired to make her wise, she took of the fruit thereof, and did eat; and gave also unto her husband with her, and he did eat.—Genesis 3:11

That this event symbolizes the breakthrough into moral conscience is clearly evident in the description which immediately follows: "The eyes of them both were opened, and they knew that they had been naked" (Genesis 3:12). Here the difference between perfection and innocence is graphically shown. The story does not portray Adam and Eve living perfectly; rather they had been living innocently until, through their human freedom, they actualized the possibility of that freedom. As a result their eyes were opened and some things they had innocently been doing they could no longer continue without guilt. Adam and Eve became morally aware. They became candidates for repenting and changing their way of life. They felt the pangs of guilt because moral awareness was based on their sense of right and wrong as it was defined by God. Becoming morally aware is becoming aware of God and the nature of his purposes in creation.

When Adam and Eve sensed this moral imperative for life and measured themselves against it they felt guilt and hid themselves from God. This is symbolic of the separation and estrangement which take place when humans sense the great distance between what they are and what with God they can be.

Confronted by God

The story also illustrates the alibis and excuses people make for their wrongdoing and the rationalization they concoct to convince themselves that their actions are not their fault. Nevertheless Adam and Eve could not go back. They had yielded an element which would forever drive them from the garden of their innocence into the world which we call the human predicament. Symbolically and realistically, the story related elements of that hard existence and estrangement to the perplexities of having to work in the midst of natural forces of destruction. This was related to eking out a livelihood, the suffering of childbearing, and the phenomenon of death.

In Conclusion

Human estrangement with its separation of the person from God, from other persons, and from the environment of earth has been viewed by Christians as the Fall. The Adam and Eve story is seen as a symbolic presentation by ancient writers to provide sense and meaning to the universal human predicament. It is not a one-time literal story of two people, but it may be applied to the development of the human race or to persons as they grow from the innocence of infancy to mature accountability. It is a story without time or place, a story of anxious, finite persons becoming aware that ultimately they cannot save themselves, that they are wholly dependent upon God.

The predicament of the Fall is not the end of the story. It merely gives meaning to the intent of Christ who, with full understanding of the cost of human creation, committed himself in the scriptural affirmation, "Father, thy will be done, and the glory be thine for ever" (Genesis 3:3).

STUDY HELPS

1. The human situation calls out for definition and yet people tend to see themselves as unfulfilled. What does the Fall mean in your life? In the lives of others?

What does your understanding of the Fall suggest about how you are called to respond?

2. If the Fall is the "transition from the perfection in the mind of God to our estranged existence," describe how humanity could have avoided it. How is such a Fall, as described in the Garden of Eden story, inherent in your creation as a free person?
3. What does *freedom* mean? Is it the same as *agency?* What does *accountability* mean? Define these three words. Then discuss how they are similar or different. How are these characteristics related to the Fall?
4. Linus, in a *Peanuts* cartoon, suggested that "nothing is so difficult as great potential." As God's creations, people are invested with magnificent potential. How and why does the author refer to this potential as "our awesome weight of freedom"?
5. Is moral concern an inherited characteristic or is it learned? If learned, when does innocence die? What does the author mean by "losing that innocence through actualizing the experience"? What is meant when the Saints say that children need not be baptized until the age of accountability? What does this have to do with the idea of the innocence of a child?
6. Persons are involved in what Ralph Perry calls the "egocentric predicament," which means they find the world centered about them. Recognizing that this is not true in most respects, it would be helpful to consider the degree to which all things people know are known in a very private world of their own experience. Can a person really understand what another is feeling? Why? Why not?
7. The Adam and Eve story is a potential parable for understanding humanity's own moral awareness. What is the distinction between your own concepts of perfection and innocence? How does the Adam and Eve story illustrate the difference between these two concepts?

CHAPTER

CHRIST AND HUMAN REDEMPTION

When considering the plight of earth-born people in their state of estrangement, we must conclude that their predicament is one from which they have no means of escape. Their gift of agency provides a finite freedom which not only makes them aware of their condition but also causes them to be God's most cruel, destructive, arrogant, and exploitive creation. At the same time the human person experiences and gives intense love, caring nurture, and sacrificial devotion and has the capacity to apprehend the eternal. Persons are a mixture of many drives, motives, and actions. The contemplation out of which deeds arise is the legacy of agency which none can escape. The noble and holy only make the satanic stand out in bolder relief. We share with the author of Isaiah who, in the presence of the Holy, exclaimed, "Woe is me! for I am undone; because I am a man of unclean lips, and I dwell in the midst of a people of unclean lips; for mine eyes have seen the King, the Lord of hosts" (Isaiah 6:5).

This Fall is often seen as a curse and some come to the conclusion that God is to be blamed. If this were the end, one could say that surely a loving God could not create humankind for such an ironic and diabolical existence. In scripture the inevitable consequence of fallen humanity is thus attributed to Satan: "For he knew not the mind of God; wherefore, he sought to destroy the world" (Genesis 3:7). Today people confront the stark reality that left to purely human devices the destruction of the world and of humanity will be literally fulfilled.

The Risk

The dilemma has been stated in chapter 8. Without the capacity to choose evil there is no capacity to choose righteousness and glory. Without the power to be satanic there can be no power to become sons and daughters of God.

We do not blame God for the human plight. We praise him. As creator, God gave the gift and accepted the risk. He chose from the beginning of creation to bear the personal cost of identifying himself with humanity and accompanying each person through the conditions of estrangement. God committed himself to pay the price to redeem the human race. People have no merits of their own entitling them to make demands on God. Yet they have been the recipients of God's grace beyond all power to describe. This grace is mediated to all humanity in God's own mighty act of redemption. The Creator entered into his creation in the person of Jesus Christ, his Only Begotten Son. God shouldered all of the conditions of estranged humanity, and personally identified with the human race to usher in the "new age," the kingdom of God. This is the age of universal regeneration—the age in which there is opened to every person the way, the power, and the understanding to become "new creatures in Christ." The concept of new persons who are regenerated presupposes old persons who were estranged. Such an assurance led the author of the Colossian letter to write:

> Now ye also put off all these; anger, wrath, malice, blasphemy, filthy communication out of your mouth. Lie not one to another, seeing that ye have put off the old man with his deeds; and have put on the new man, which is renewed in knowledge after the image of him that created him.—Colossians 3:8-10

The "new man" is in the image of God. Christ is the first of the new humanity into which all people are called.

The Meaning of Christ

When God entered into his creation of time and space in the person of Jesus he became "God with us" (Matthew 2:6). This is the message so often heard at Christmastime. The concept is both overwhelming and unfathomable. We struggle for words to express our understanding but even then we are aware that our thoughts are inadequate and our knowledge the mere tip of the iceberg. The known is very small compared to the unknown. The vast area of the unfathomed is the mystery which adds to our awe. Our faith can never be adamantly stated, as if we know all there is to consider. We fall far short when we discuss the meaning of Christ. Our attitude must be characterized by humility rather than brashness or arrogance.

Christ as Mediator

The Christian faith leads us to affirm that Christ is the mediator. He bridges the gulf between the finite, estranged race and the perfection of the eternal God. Christ is that one who shares with every person the conditions of existence, even to death on the cross, but he is not overcome by those conditions. By making the "word flesh," God gives to all persons the hope and assurance that they can be redeemed and reunited with the eternal or spiritual reality from which they each have their source of being.

Mediation is not only victory over the power of evil and death; it is reunion with life and the eternal reality. For Christians this is the gift of eternal life. By saying that Christ is the first of the new age or that he ushers in the new age, we are describing who and what he is.

When speaking of him as redeemer and savior, we affirm that through him we have the power to enter into the new age with him and inherit eternal life.

The idea of a mediator or mediators is not limited to the Christian faith; many religions entertain such a belief. Generally the ideas of mediator gods emerge when the greatest god reaches a point of abstraction which removes him from access to the people. Then the people create images of lesser gods and holy people to mediate for them. In paganism the mediator gods are lower than the chief god and subject to his control. Some Christian people have developed such ideas. They have reasoned that God is so great that they must approach him through Jesus. It may then seem that Jesus, the Son of God, is so far removed that he should be approached through some highly regarded human, living or dead, who is supposedly more holy than they.

The Concept of the Son of God

While this chain of mediation has had some place in the thought of Christian groups, it is contrary to our best understanding of faith. We declare that Christ is not less than God nor is he unapproachable. The Apostle Paul wrote, "Let this mind be in you, which was also in Christ Jesus; who, being in the form of God, thought it not robbery to be equal with God" (Philippians 2:5, 6). This is the meaning of being "the Only Begotten Son of God." The human or divine mind creates that which is less than or of a lower order than the mind which created it. That which is begotten, however, is of an order equal to its parents. When speaking of Jesus Christ as the "Only Begotten Son of God" we are declaring him to be of the same order as God.

On one concept everyone agrees: God cannot cease to be God. It is incorrect, therefore, to take such terms as "God became man" too literally. God does not become something other than God. To keep human concepts accurate, the common practice has been to speak of "Jesus the Christ," the "Messiah," or the "Son of God." This understanding must be carried in concert with the awareness that Jesus was also fully human. This Christian concept does not imagine some third order of reality. For the purposes of this consideration we know of only two orders of reality. These are the order of the eternal and the order of created existence. He who represents God and humankind is not half God and half human. Such a new third order of reality could represent neither God nor human. As Christians we affirm that Christ is fully God and fully human. This is possible when Christ, who is that person representing the perfection from which we all have fallen, comes into our midst as the "new man" who lives with us under the conditions of our existence but is not conquered by those conditions. Christ is the perfect human, the one without sin. Jesus Christ is the person from that order of reality which is eternal.

The Concept of the "New Age" in Christ

For Christ to be the "new man" embodying the eternal is to say that in him dwelt the essential Godness of God and also the eternal spiritual quality of humankind. Both are of the order of the eternal. Thus they are not two different realities but one joined in the person Jesus Christ.

The concept of the unity of God and humanity expressed in Christ will always be imperfectly stated and understood by estranged persons. When finite minds press the idea they always find it shading into unexplained mystery. This is because our experience in time and space does not equip us to delve deeply into the reality of the eternal.

The Christian Paradox

Much of society views the Christian faith as a paradox. This means that it contradicts human opinion which has been formed in the context of the estrangement of the human predicament. In this context in the Gospel of John, Jesus said, "If the world hate you, ye know that it hated me before it hated you" (John 15:18), and prayed for his disciples, "I have given them thy word; and the world hath hated them, because they are not of the world, even as I am not of the world" (John 17:14). The evidence of this antagonism may be encountered at any place in the world of estranged people. Those who live in nations of a predominately Christian culture, however, do not fully understand the intensity of opposition that is commonly encountered by faithful Christian people who live in non-Christian cultures.

For the Jews of Jesus' time the claims of Jesus could be seen only as blasphemy: one who was known as a common and uneducated man from Nazareth was usurping authority and power which belonged to God. Even more heretical from the standpoint of their background was his claim to fulfill and supersede the law, which was for them the fruit of the mighty acts of God in delivering the law through Moses.

While the Jews looked for a Messiah, they expected his role to be that of the great leader and spokesman for God who would establish the nation in glory to fulfill its cosmic mission. After Jesus' death Christians read such Old Testament writings as Isaiah's prophecy of the "suffering servant" believing they foretold the mission of Christ. Jews, however, had always read it as indicating the mission of their race as God's chosen people.

This basic difference in belief between the early Christians and the Jews brought these two concepts into confrontation. If the Christians had been willing to continue to accept the supremacy of the law, Christianity would have become one of the many Jewish sects. Christians understood the Christ to be the "new man" whose victorious life had opened the way to eternal life and who, through his continuing spiritual presence, had lifted them out of the estrangement of existence into the glorious liberty of sons and daughters of God. They could not allow the law to claim their allegiance. Adherence to the law could not be a prerequisite to Christian fellowship. The Apostle Paul was the adamant speaker for this position. He stated the case strongly in his letter to the congregation in Rome:

> For what the law could not do, in that it was weak through the flesh, God sending his own Son in the likeness of sinful flesh, and for sin, condemned sin in the flesh; that the righteousness of the law might be fulfilled in us, who walk not after the flesh, but after the Spirit.—Romans 8:3, 4

In Conclusion

It is the lot of fallen human beings always to strive to be their own saviors and struggle to find fulfillment at the expense of other people and the resources of creation. The inevitable consequence is that their efforts entangle them in greater estrangement, guilt, and anxiety. Persons do this individually and corporately, as in nationalism when they elevate their country to be their highest value. In the past century science was elevated by some societies and named the savior of humanity. It was thought that all human problems would eventually yield to scientific knowledge and power. The decade of the 1960s was perhaps the moment of truth when great numbers of people began to understand that scientific knowledge utilized by estranged and self-serving society was not a savior. It was instead creating a world which could destroy itself.

When people try to save themselves they often grasp hold of some object, institution, or method within the realm of time and space. This provides for them the security and fulfillment of a savior. Yet in doing so they have chosen to put their faith in an idol. In modern times this may be wealth, the strength of the nation, the technology and method of science, or some other supposed power. Whatever the idol, it always fails the ones who trust it. The reality of time and space does not create itself nor does it have the power to save itself. This reality is characterized by estrangement and its salvation must come from outside itself. It must come from the reality of the eternal. God, not the human race, is the source of salvation.

Jesus Christ was the Son of God who is the eternal order of reality. In redeeming the world he became a part of estranged existence without being overcome by estrangement. Jesus Christ became the "new man" in the "new age" to usher in the kingdom of God. He is therefore the redeemer of the world to lift it into that perfection which dwelt in the mind of God and is God's intent in the purposes of creation.

STUDY HELPS

1. Dury suggests that "if you would live more lives than one you must be willing to die more deaths than one." What does this statement say to you? How is this related to the author's assurance that there is risk in becoming a child of God? What are the risks? What is the price to be paid?
2. You or another class member might read again chapter 2 of *Exploring the Faith*, pages 30-51. What are the main ideas that the statement presents about Jesus Christ? How does this statement relate to the author's views? How do your beliefs agree or disagree with *Exploring the Faith?* Why?

3. Human beings are offered the opportunity to be "new creatures in Christ." Yet to do so people must put away their old selves. What does this imply about "being ourselves"? How is this a call to lose oneself? What degree is it a call for renewal?
4. Describe to another class member a personal experience when you felt you became a new creature in Christ. How did you change?
5. What is meant by the statement, "If the world hate you, ye know that it hated me before it hated you"? How does this reflect ministry?
6. Look up the term *mediator* in a dictionary. If you can, also locate a copy of the *Fair Labor Standards Act* or its equivalent for another country. In both cases there is a clear definition of the mediator that differs from that used by the author when he refers to Christ. Take time to discover why this different use is valid.
7. What is required of humanity with Christ as mediator? Do people negotiate with God? Why? Why not? Before answering think about your creation as a free person and evaluate your behavior seriously. How is mediation used here to mean more than only one who intervenes?
8. Why may Jesus' repeated comment to his disciples that he was "not of the world" interfere with today's understanding of his humanity? How is the distinction between being *in* the world and *of* the world significant in understanding the author's views on "the Christian paradox"?
9. What is this chapter's relationship to chapter 4? Reread those parts of chapter 4 that relate to Christ's role among the people of God.

CHAPTER 10

THE MIRROR OF THE CROSS

All humans are a complex mixture of characteristics which include a wide range from good to evil. They are selfish and at the same time they give themselves in selfless sacrifice for others. They may be both vain and humble, cruel and kind, anxious and well-controlled. It is impossible for even one individual to identify the many motives and crosscurrents of desire, fear, and guilt that influence a decision to act. Much of the time persons hide from other people motives which they feel are evil or unworthy, but they also hide those motives from themselves. They do this by rationalizing—convincing themselves that others do things as bad or worse—or by laying the blame on others. As we measure ourselves against this temporal world and the estranged people in it, we may feel justified in our actions.

At this point the events surrounding the crucifixion shock us out of our complacency to see the awfulness of the sin we harbor within ourselves. We may also see the glory of our potential in creation. While we stand in awe before the cross as a historical event, we are stricken as we see ourselves in the people who participated in that drama. It is the story of all estranged persons. Our lives and motives are revealed, from the highest to the lowest.

While the profound significance of the event is never fully understood by mortals, some of the meanings do strike with amazing force.

Human Fickleness

During the short period of the ministry of Jesus crowds of people flocked to hear and see him. The scriptures called them the "multitudes." On one occasion when such a great company gathered on the mountainside and there seemed to be insufficient food, Jesus fed all the people from five barley loaves and two small fishes a lad had brought along for lunch. The miracle so enthralled the crowds that Jesus left to keep them from taking him by force to make him their king (John 6:15). This was an example of his popularity which appears to have reached its zenith at the time of his triumphal entry into Jerusalem. This entry marked the beginning of that last week which included his crucifixion.

Although the crowds that gathered on the various occasions described in the scriptures were not composed of exactly the same people, it is fairly certain that large numbers of them were the same individuals. In this light it seems almost unthinkable that a multitude could have changed so much just a week after they had strewed palm leaves on the road before him and cried, "Hosanna! Blessed is he that cometh in the name of the Lord; that bringeth the kingdom of our father David; blessed is he that cometh in the name of the Lord; Hosanna in the highest" (Mark 11:10-12). Many of the same people who had proclaimed him king appeared ready to crucify him before the week was over. When Pilate reminded them that they had called him "King of the Jews," they "cried out again, Deliver him unto us to be crucified. Away with him. Crucify him" (Mark 15:14, 15). They were the people who watched unfeelingly as he was nailed to the cross, who taunted him as he suffered in agony. They mocked him and said, "Ah, thou who destroyest the temple and buildest it in three days, save thyself, and come down from the cross" (Mark 15:34).

We may be moved by feelings of disgust and anger toward those who were so fickle, who rose from the heights of honoring their Savior to the depths of human cruelty. Many say, "How could they do that?"

At this point we all need to turn our thoughts inward. The characteristics we view with such horror in the crowds that gathered to crucify Jesus are in us and our society. In a short time nations and people who have welcomed each other in warm friendliness are brought to war and hatred. Persons whose race or ancestry clearly identifies them as residents of the hated nation may receive cruel treatment or find their lives jeopardized. Hatred is easily generated toward persons who are different politically, economically, or religiously. The tabulation of our fickle ways is a never-ending list. We are so easily turned from love to hatred, from praise to denigration, from doing good to doing evil. Amazingly such wickedness parades under the banner of good. We rationalize our attitudes and actions so that we seem good. We say we are saving the nation, our social system, our religious beliefs, or our personal honor.

Our motives are not really clear even to ourselves. When we are as honest as we can be, we know that our motives are sometimes influenced by self-interest—employment, prestige, position in society, or the success of the class, nation, or religion. Sometimes we are influenced by our desire to be popular and accepted. We are often moved by our own self-righteousness. Sometimes we are genuinely convinced that the situation requires the type of action in which the needs of the few must be sacrificed for the welfare of the many. Dealing with these problems in a complex world is not easy.

Personal Fear

Fear was probably an element in much of the drama of Jesus' crucifixion. One of the persons whose actions strike at the core of human nature is Simon Peter. He sincerely thought his allegiance to Jesus was unshakable. When the soldiers took Jesus prisoner, Peter drew his sword, ready to do battle for the safety of his Master. When Jesus on a prior occasion had told this strong man that he had prayed especially for him that his "faith fail not," Peter had been hurt and had staunchly declared, "Lord, I am ready to go with you, both into prison, and unto death" (Luke 22:32, 33).

Peter, however, did not know himself. Perhaps he would have gone down fighting the soldiers to protect Jesus. But when he was called to be a "new man" with Jesus, not responding in like kind to an estranged world, he could not understand and was afraid. When Jesus was led to the high priest's house "Peter followed afar off," and when a girl recognized Peter in the crowd he denied that he even knew Jesus.

The remainder of the story is well known. It is mentioned here not to belittle this staunch disciple but to admit that we, too, are like Peter. We are sometimes reluctant to admit our identity. Like Peter we use language inappropriate to our faith so that we will be more acceptable to the people of the world. We even engage in activities to hide our true feelings in order to be one of the crowd. The times others have stood fast and been counted, as was Peter in the presence of the soldiers, do not atone for the times we have denied him by acts of unfaithfulness.

The Influence of Self-interest

Consider the drama leading up to the cross and take note of the self-interest of the disciples. Even though they had spent nearly three years with Jesus they were concerned about their personal status. The mothers too got into the controversy. The scriptures indicate that on a number of occasions little jealousies crept in to hinder the work of the Master.

On one such occasion Jesus soberly informed the disciples of the tragic events to follow, including his own crucifixion. It appeared as if they were not concerned about his needs; they were too preoccupied with concerns about themselves. The mother of James and John came with her sons to ask that they be allowed to sit one on his right hand the other on his left. The sons showed that they also wanted the recognition, for in response to Jesus' question, they declared, "We are able" (Matthew 20:22).

While we might be critical of James, John, and their mother, it appears that self-interest was widely shared. In Matthew it is written, "And when the ten heard this, they were moved with indignation against the two brethren" (Matthew 20:24). The ten would not have been jealous had they not also coveted recognition.

In this situation Jesus once again found it necessary to show them what it means to be the "new person" in the "new age." He said to them all:

> Ye know that the princes of the Gentiles exercise dominion over them, and they that are great exercise authority upon them; but it shall not be so among you. But whosoever will be great among you, let him be your minister. And whosoever will be chief among you, let him be your servant; even as the Son of Man came, not to be ministered unto, but to minister; and to give his life a ransom for many.—Matthew 20:25-28

John suggests that following the Last Supper, Jesus, knowing that his hour had come, washed the feet of his disciples and said:

> Know ye what I have done to you? Ye call me Master and Lord; and ye say well; for so I am. If I then, your Lord and Master, have washed your feet, ye also ought to wash one another's feet. For I

have given you an example, that ye should do as I have done to you.—John 13:12-15

We can hardly read of these events without observing how much we too aspire to recognition, honor, and power. We get our feelings hurt and pout or refuse to participate in causes we know to be good if we think we are not sufficiently appreciated. We respond even more negatively when we are criticized. When doing something good we want credit.

Dodging Involvement

Perhaps no one other than Judas has received more disdain in the crucifixion drama than Pilate. He believed Jesus was innocent of wrongdoing and had the power to save him from the mob, but he was not brave enough to stand against pressure. He feared his opponents might use the incident to discredit him in Rome, with a resulting reprimand or even release from office. He preferred to go before the people and wash his hands of the whole affair. Let them be responsible. He chose not to be involved.

We see ourselves in this weak man. How often do we symbolically wash our hands, refusing to become involved. Others suffer injustices when we have the power to right a wrong or at least help the oppressed. We are afraid of being inconvenienced or hated by the oppressors or ostracized. It is easier not to be involved or to shift the responsibility to others.

Doing Our Job

The soldiers, as far as is known, did not dislike Jesus. They had been given orders and they had a job to do. Their task was to get it over as quickly and unfeelingly as possible. They gambled for his meager possessions while they waited. It was for them that Jesus in his agony prayed, "Father, forgive them; for they know not what they do" (Luke 23:35).

The question of personal responsibility for actions commanded by a superior is still raised in modern military discipline. Who is responsible in war crimes? The Saints are reminded of the courageous stand of Brigadier General A. W. Doniphan when he refused to carry out an order to shoot Joseph Smith and other prisoners in the public square of Far West on November 2, 1838. The question is still a perplexing one which seems deeply rooted in the nature of our estranged existence. Personal responsibility poses a problem for civilized societies.

The Agony of Love

We must not leave this consideration without remembering the little band that stayed by Jesus, sharing his anguish. They experienced indescribable suffering. Jesus' mother, Mary, certain other women, John, and perhaps others stayed by the cross. Love flowed among them and there was strength here. Joseph of Arimathea and Nicodemus, not so boldly but nevertheless lovingly, prepared the body of Christ for burial and placed it in a new sepulcher.

The drama of those last few days revealed strengths, courage, and willingness to sacrifice which also are a part of humanity. We are neither wholly bad nor wholly good, but we are daily among the crowd at the cross.

In Conclusion

When we thoughtfully consider that last week of Jesus' life and the responses of Jesus and the various people who participated in the drama, we are amazed at the power and meaning of those events. We see ourselves and our natures, from the highest to the lowest, in the people who shared in that experience.

Who of us has not been angered by people who challenged our religious and moral beliefs and who successfully convinced others of their rightness? We, too, are antagonistic toward those who advocate social changes which may overturn our position in society. When sincerely trying to understand the Pharisees who were dedicated to keeping Judaism true to the Mosaic Law and free from the heresies of foreign religions, we know that the problems of Jesus' time are still active today.

We, too, do terrible things to people whose behavior and ideas deviate from ours. We reject them as persons and use force to stop their activities and punish them. It is sobering to think that we might have been among the number that cried, "Crucify him." Like the Jews of Jesus' time, we rationalize our actions. We tell ourselves we are protecting the right way of life, the right belief, when in reality we are protecting our entrenched beliefs and social position.

We find it easy to be drawn into mass action and do things we would never initiate or do alone. We do terrible things as mobs or associations or even governments which we would not do in person-to-person relationships. The mob may have witnessed the crucifixion without any feelings of guilt. Some even share in the event by taunting Jesus in his agony. This strain in our own natures sometimes surfaces in similar ways.

We see ourselves in the disciples who followed afar off—but who did follow, and in Peter who denied Christ under fear and pressure. We see ourselves in the anguished disciples, including the women, who stood at the foot of the cross crushed by the awfulness of the day's events. We feel ourselves responding as did John when Jesus asked him to care for his mother.

We cannot here explore in depth the many ways in

which various persons who participated in that week's drama reveal the many sides of our own personalities. Yet we must understand that it was not just the people of Jesus' time who crucified him. All of us—by our sin, lack of allegiance, weakness of character, wavering faith—crucify the Christ. But this is only part of the drama, for we also respond to the good, the right, and the noble. We sometimes maintain tremendous fidelity to Jesus Christ and his purposes. We are a mixture of all the elements portrayed by those people involved in that crucial week. In those complex actions, Jesus teaches us so much about ourselves that we must stand in awe, repentance, joy, and hope.

The most important person of that week, however, was Jesus. In him was revealed the nature of God in most bold and piercing ways. Having looked at ourselves as we really are, we see in Jesus the understanding, compassionate, forgiving yet unyielding nature of the "new man." He revealed the eternal to which we all are called.

Jesus knew Peter was not strong enough to withstand the fear of being linked with him as the mob grew tense. Yet Jesus loved him; and the angels at the sepulcher took special note of Peter's needs when, after the resurrection, they asked the women at the tomb to "tell his disciples and Peter." Without doubt Peter felt unworthy and condemned by his denial of Christ.

Jesus was concerned about his disciples and the work he had begun. In the struggle before his suffering, he prayed for his followers. He promised to be with his disciples to the end of time.

Even the soldiers who crucified Jesus were in his prayers and concern. When he looked on them from his own death struggles he prayed the Father to forgive them for, he said, "they know not what they do" (Luke 23:35).

Jesus had counseled his hearers saying, "Love your enemies; bless them that curse you; do good to them that hate you; and pray for them that despitefully use you and persecute you" (Matthew 5:46). While such counsel had seemed visionary and impractical before, it suddenly was validated in a life given for all.

The question is not so much, "What might have been done then?" In light of our Christian faith, born out of the memory of the drama, the question becomes, "What shall we as Christ's followers do now?" That is a humbling and perplexing question and a persistent one.

We shall fall short of our eternal calling, and as we do we can be grateful for the grace of God that continues to support us. That grace is our hope and will not let us take our ease. There is a calling which is attained only in eternal life.

The Christian victory is not in the fact that we shall fall short of the mark; God is not finished with us yet. The victory is in the assurance that we can attain. Christ has come and we will triumph. This is the promise.

STUDY HELPS

1. Why would people have been afraid of Jesus? How would you have reacted if you had been in the crowd that followed Jesus from praise to crucifixion? Why?
2. One of the great mysteries of Christ's eventful moment in history is how one can be master and slave, weak yet strong, disciple yet antagonist. What are the possibilities of being master through service? What is required of a person who is both master and slave?
3. What is the role of congregational leaders in light of

the preceding question? How may they be both master and slave?

4. Describe the great conflict that existed between Pilate's potential aid to Jesus and his commission to "let the people decide" according to the laws of Rome. What conflicts might there be among soldiers who followed their bond to obey their master? Often choice is not between good and bad but between seemingly equal negative possibilities. How might you be torn between the good of meeting commitments and the good of family relationships? How might you respond to the evil of killing and the evil of refusing to support your country in times of need? How might several responses be Christian in nature?
5. In Jesus' plea, "Father, forgive them; for they know not what they do," is he speaking of the soldiers' innocence or lack of moral awareness? Why was there no prayer offered for Judas? Write a prayer on behalf of Judas. What aims motivated him?
6. Why is the crucifixion always celebrated as a victory? How is this a victory for God? How was it a victory for you?
7. Several class members may read chapter 17 in *Exploring the Faith*, pages 216-225. Plan a panel presentation with the class discussing key points about the meaning of the Resurrection.
8. With which of the characters attending Jesus' arrest, trial, and crucifixion do you most closely identify? Why? Which personal strengths and weaknesses does this comparison bring out?

CHAPTER 11

CHRIST IN ATONEMENT

Throughout the centuries devoted Christians have sensed a meaning in Jesus' sacrificial life which goes beyond his function as a teacher, healer, or leader. These functions do not clearly satisfy the person who raises the question, *why?* Humanity stands before the cross in awe and asks, Why has almighty God done this for us? Why was it necessary? Their theories have been set out in the doctrine of the atonement.

The atonement inevitably shades off into the mystery of God's eternal nature and the expression of his commitment to redeem humanity. Persons who grapple with these questions know they find depths they cannot plumb. The explanations given have been framed in the legal and social customs of the societies concerned. They are attempts to answer the question why in a way which makes sense to people. Therefore the answers given in one cultural context have been different from those developed in another. If people take any of the theories literally, as a complete and authoritative explanation for all time, they will end up with erroneous concepts and the explanations will in time make less and less sense. Many persons today find the explanations of the past quite unsatisfactory.

Theories of Atonement

Christians have held four major theories about the nature and purpose of the atonement. They have explained the atonement in ways that made sense in their time and in their cultures.

The first major explanation of the atonement, sometimes called the Latin theory, was set forth by Anselm. Essentially it is legalistic, holding that Jesus through his death on the cross earned an excess of merit which is paid to God as a compensation for human sin. This payment was required because the human race, being sinful, was unable to make an adequate recompense. Redemption was not possible unless God sent his Son as the sinless perfect human to satisfy the debt. God did through Jesus Christ what humankind could not do to make redemption possible.

The second theory of the atonement is sometimes called the sacrificial interpretation. It is a theory often based on the book of Hebrews. Like Anselm's Latin theory, it presumes that the fallen race cannot redress its own sin and guilt. A vicarious sacrifice is therefore required. In a symbolic sense the "blood of the Lamb" saves the people; Jesus is the innocent person who died for all. Through this vicarious act Jesus the man sacrificed himself for all people. This act appeased God's wrath. In this way justice is maintained and God's relationship of love for humankind is reestablished.

A third interpretation of the doctrine of atonement is the subjective theory. It came into being with the concerns of the social reformers of the nineteenth century. The promoters of this theory believed that the idea of God's wrath was inconsistent with his unconditional love. They taught that the idea of Jesus making a sacrifice to appease God is false.

Those who believed in the subjective theory felt that Jesus Christ's noble commitment to the principles of life which led to his crucifixion was the means through which God acted to inspire believing persons to a new and higher moral life. The love of God manifest in Jesus

Christ even under the conditions of the crucifixion helps persons to understand that the universe is basically friendly. God, the author of creation, continues to support and direct the affairs of people as a God of love, not wrath. The atonement, therefore, is God's moral support and victorious example to give persons hope, confidence, and faith to become the children of God.

The fourth theory of the atonement is the classical interpretation. Many worthy Christian leaders such as the Apostle Paul and Martin Luther have given this meaning to Christ's atonement. They have believed that God's love led him to come in the person of Jesus Christ to reveal to humans the truth that life has purpose and meaning. Jesus' trial, death, and resurrection help believing persons to see that evil and death do not, in the long run, win over righteousness and life. Victory is guaranteed in the revealed truth of Jesus Christ. Human existence is not a tragic affair ending in an ironic failure.

God has taken the initiative to show persons the real nature of life. To demonstrate his never-ending love, God assumed the role of the "suffering servant" and identified with humanity, even to the point of suffering the worst that sinful people could do to him—death. Jesus suffered the defeat of death to help people see that because God is the giver of life, death and evil can never win.

In the atonement Christ clearly demonstrated the loving restraint characteristic of the almighty God who could have destroyed the wicked or overwhelmed the tormentors of Jesus by divine power. In Matthew's account, Peter tried to defend Jesus with the sword. Jesus said, "Thinkest thou that I cannot now pray to my Father, and he shall presently give me more than twelve legions of angels?" (Matthew 26:51). God's commitment is one of love. Since the love of God begets love in the hearts of persons which raises them to the nature of the new being, it was necessary for God's love to shine forth in this divine act for all humanity to see.

The Essential Nature of Atonement

While the interpretations of the atonement developed in the past are in certain aspects unsatisfactory, valuable insights are provided by each interpretation. We do not presume that the modern world gives a final interpretation which is free from cultural limitations. As long as estranged humans live in a temporal world they will find the explanation of the atonement shrouded in mystery.

There are some principles, however, that may guide our understanding. First, we must approach the meaning of the atonement as an explanation of Jesus' acts to transform estranged persons into "new beings." Those who have been grasped by the power of the atonement may feel the totality of God's atoning grace in their lives as they experience this "rebirth." They may not, however, be able to put all that they comprehend into words. Theirs is a total experience which involves more than intellect and therefore is not fully communicated or understood by it. It is the kind of unique transformation which made the early saints say, "The world knoweth us not, because it knew him not" (I John 3:1).

Christians must accept this principle with a great deal of humility. A truth which has a certain exclusiveness can easily become the excuse for developing a shallow elitism. Those who feel they have achieved a certain level of experience not understood by others often withdraw from society and feel superior to people whom they consider to be ignorant. The net effect of such feelings is the attitude of the Pharisee: "God, I thank thee that I am not as other men" (Luke 18:11).

Such an attitude takes on the symbols and language of the reborn in Christ, but it deceives the persons involved. They have slipped back into the world of estrangement and have lost the new life without knowing it is gone. They are described by Jesus:

> Many will say unto me in that day, Lord, Lord, have we not prophesied in thy name; and in thy name cast out devils; and in thy name done many wonderful works? And then will I say, Ye never knew me; depart from me ye that work iniquity.—Matthew 7:32, 33

By saying that the atonement is an explanation of Christ's acts to transform estranged persons from their fallen condition into new or reborn persons, we are describing Christ's awesome sacrifice to bring humankind back into unity with the eternal or to become at one with God.

The error in human thinking sometimes emerges at the point where people argue that God's anger must be assuaged and his attitude changed to goodwill toward humanity. It is misleading to teach that the sin of the human race so offended God that humankind could not do anything which would be an adequate recompense for the grievous sin committed in "the Fall." God is not angry with the human race, nor has he been. We believe that the act of Christ does not change God. This mighty act changes humanity. Paul says it more clearly in the statement, "God is in Christ, reconciling the world unto himself, not imputing their trespasses unto them; and hath committed unto us the word of reconciliation" (II Corinthians 5:19). Rather than God needing to be reconciled, it was the world, which includes humanity, that needs to be reconciled.

Overcoming the Separation from Guilt

Christ's atonement overcomes the estrangement of persons from God by removing the unsurmountable factor of human guilt. The consciousness of guilt drives persons to hide from God. This is symbolized in the Garden of Eden story when Adam and Eve hid from the divine presence because they knew they were disobedient. Through Christ persons come to recognize that they may be forgiven if they are willing to accept the divine offer of reconciliation. This is symbolized particularly in the sacraments. The amazing principle of the atoning process is extended to persons through the act of God. Reconciliation is not possible by personal merit but by the grace of God who loves all. Even children who have disobeyed their parents cannot be fully reconciled to the parents until they know the cleansing power of forgiveness.

God is not dependent on Christ to act as a go-between. Rather Christ, the "New Man," is the bearer of God's reconciling power to humankind.

Love and Justice

The justice of God is not personal vengeance designed to punish the sinner. God's nature is that of unconditional love. God's love was not learned through a conditioning process. We are conditioned by the impact of our environment—we love other persons because we have been related to them in circumstances which evoke love. For instance, babies are conditioned to love their mothers. We may be conditioned in the same way to hate.

God is not as he is because we have made him that way. God alone is unconditioned. The Creator is as he is because he is God. When speaking of God's unconditional love, we admit that God loves humanity because he is God and not because we have done some great thing to cause him to love.

God's justice, however, must be seen not only in terms of what his love demands for our welfare, but also for the welfare of all creation. God lets the self-destructive consequences of estrangement work their course. They are a part of the nature of creation. If God removed these consequences he would contradict his own creation and cease to be a God of order or even of love itself. Justice is the expression of love in natural law and, without this, love would be weak sentimentality. Justice is God's structural exercise of love, resisting and destroying the evil which is against love. There is no opposition or conflict between strong justice and strong love in the divine economy.

Forgiveness and Estrangement

The tendency toward a shallow interpretation of the atonement is an ever-present human problem, often seen in the theology of humanism. Forgiveness requires a mutual sharing of the offense. In a sense one who forgives shares the guilt and burden of sin. This is not some casual matter. God pays a price to identify with human beings and accept the burden of guilt with them. In the atonement Christ identifies with our estranged circumstances and carries our burden, but he is not overcome by those conditions.

Sin is not something separate or apart from the sinner. The person rebels against God; therefore, the person must be forgiven and brought to repentance. God's unconditional love guarantees that he is always waiting for his children to turn from rebellion and ask for help. When the burden of sin is laid at the feet of Jesus, our faith grants assurance that God accepts the burden of the sin. The cost of atonement is not some easily made decision on God's part to cancel or wipe out an obligation. It is the cost of sharing the burden of estrangement and is experienced by persons who accept God's power to overcome their estrangement. God frees all. We need not continue in sin but are called to become new persons in Christ. This is God's intent for his creation.

Atonement and Consequences

The corrective expression of God's love which is structured into natural law is not removed by God's forgiveness. Those self-destructive consequences are not erased by the atonement. Rather Christ has participated with humanity in the temporal creation, taking on himself the circumstances of the human predicament and transforming life for all who share his temporal participation. The parent who forgives a disobedient child reestablishes the relationship which was broken if the child accepts the forgiveness. But this forgiveness does not wipe out the consequences of the wrongdoing.

The Trial, Crucifixion, and Resurrection

Christ's victorious participation in the estranged temporal world and his incorporation of the destructive elements of that arrogant world in his life are clearly shown in the week of the trial, crucifixion, and resurrection. When looking at the trial and the cross, we sense the forces of hate, self-entrenchment, political power, and rebellion against God building to a crescendo. Jesus accepted the brunt of all these destructive powers and participated in the most feared of all the conditions of the temporal world—death. In doing so, he did not vary from the eternal order of reality. He did not hate his tormentors. He prayed God's forgiveness on the soldiers. He told his disciple not to use force to defend him. No place is the "new being" so meaningfully portrayed as in the drama of that week. While the world was in a frenzy, Jesus presided over the events in which he participated.

On that first Easter morn, as the meaning of the

Resurrection began to work in the minds and hearts of Jesus' followers, it became clear that he had transformed the circumstances. Death, evil, and self-destruction were never to be feared again. These forces were conquered in the person of Jesus Christ. All who participate with him know that victory has been won through the atonement made by God's Only Begotten Son.

In Conclusion

The atonement must not be seen as some ransom paid to Satan to release humanity from a satanic grip. Whatever connotation one places on the term *redemption*, it is not a price paid to Satan to buy back the human race, but rather the price paid to lift us from our estrangement into the reality of new being. The atonement is a return to the eternal reality which was in the mind of God universally and focused in Christ. Jesus Christ specifically overcame the circumstances of our temporal estranged existence. Christ transforms us into new beings if we accept him. This transformation is the gift of eternal life.

STUDY HELPS

1. The author explains some of the more widely held views of the atonement. Consider these in light of the following questions: (a) Why did God have to be compensated for human sin? (b) In what way is it just for an innocent person to be sacrificed (as was Christ) for all persons? (c) What did Christ expect as a result of his death?
2. It is traditional to see atonement as at-one-ment. What does this view tell you about the meaning of

Christ's sacrifice on the cross?

3. You and several other class members may appreciate reading chapter 45 in Elton Trueblood's *Confronting Christ* (Harper and Row, 1960). Summarize Trueblood's views and lead the class in a discussion about the Divine Transformation. What does this term mean? How does it occur? When have you felt it?
4. Look up several Old Testament and New Testament references which comment on the author's view that "God is not angry with the human race, nor has he been."
5. Many persons say they do not want God's justice (for they know what they deserve) but rather his mercy (for they know what they seek). How are justice and mercy combined in the concept of the atonement?
6. In light of the preceding question, construct some ideas on how, though atonement occurs and forgiveness follows, the consequences of behavior remain.
7. Karl Barth has suggested that the nature of the atonement is such that the Judge is judged in humanity's place, but that it was not done to satisfy the wrath of God. How is this similar or different from what the author has said?
8. What impact has Christ's sacrifice made on you? Describe how your life has been changed by God's never-ending love.

CHAPTER 12

FACING UP TO EVIL

Christian faith never flinches when it confronts the hard realities of tragedy. The world has never been a place of ease for its inhabitants, and crisis is a characteristic of life. Death is universal, and persons every day confront disaster in such common ways as the hazards of travel, the suffering of disease, the violence of crime, or the results of famine and poverty. Perhaps the most ghastly possibilities have been reserved for modern times as the world is threatened by war's grim atomic holocaust or even greater destructive consequences of newer weapons of annihilation. In the midst of human invention the power of self-destruction looms ever more ominous.

People who face the issues of life realistically do not want a faith which denies the tragedy they see in the world around them. They cannot ignore the suffering or take refuge in some isolated station which protects them from pain.

Some groups of people seem to have lost their sense of meaning and rush to gather the flowers of life lest they miss the thrill if they wait until tomorrow. Moral values and integrity are all too often discarded. Responsibility for one's self and other people is sacrificed in the name of personal rights.

Some people avoid facing life by filling their hours with entertainment and social activities, some through the use of alcohol and drugs, some with a kind of emotional religion which creates for them an unreal world that exists only in imagination. Many are living beyond their means in ways which involve much more than money.

No Promise of Ease

None of these escapes are worthy of honest living. Jesus did not promise his followers such an unreal world. He did not encourage the people to believe that accepting his way would insulate them from difficulty.

When Jesus taught about the values of faith, he did not lead people to think God turned trials away from those who obeyed the gospel. To the contrary he said, "And he who taketh not his cross and followeth after me, is not worthy of me" (Matthew 10:33). When he was concluding that great statement of the gospel known as "The Sermon on the Mount" he said:

> Therefore, whosoever heareth these sayings of mine and doeth them, I will liken him unto a wise man, who built his house upon a rock, and the rains descended, and the floods came, and the winds blew, and beat upon that house, and it fell not; for it was founded upon a rock.
>
> And every one that heareth these sayings of mine, and doeth them not, shall be likened unto a foolish man, who built his house upon the sand; and the rains descended, and the floods came, and the winds blew, and beat upon that house, and it fell; and great was the fall of it.—Matthew 7:34, 35

The man who built his house upon a rock was not spared the rains and floods. The same winds blew and beat on his house as those which buffeted the house built upon the sand. The difference between the two houses was in the foundation on which they rested. So it is with human life. The person with a firm faith in God has an inner strength not possessed by those without faith.

This view of life does not promise escape from the hard realities encountered by all people. We do God injustice by implying that obedience to him guarantees his goodwill, and that we will be spared the evil which tests others. It is true, of course, that persons who disregard the laws of good health or sound management of their stewardship or moral integrity suffer some results which may not come to one who lives by the principles of the gospel. These principles are in harmony with the nature of God's creation. Nevertheless, history and personal experience are replete with instances where the innocent suffer while the guilty go unpunished, where righteousness is trampled under the brute force of greed and power. Sometimes it is difficult not to draw the conclusion that evil succeeds while good is trodden underfoot.

The Dream of a Perfect Society

Significantly, the human race has dreamed since the days of antiquity of a society of universal peace and prosperity. The Jews lived by such a dream. Their prophets had spoken of a time when the nations

> shall beat their swords into ploughshares, and their spears into pruning-hooks; nation shall not lift up a sword against nation, neither shall they learn war any more. But they shall sit every man under his vine and under his fig tree; and none shall make them afraid; for the mouth of the Lord of hosts hath spoken it.—Micah 4:3, 4

It is of interest to note that prophecy of Tennyson in "Locksley Hall":

> Till the war-drum throbb'd no longer, and the battle-flags were furl'd
> In Parliament of man, the Federation of the world.
> There the common sense of most shall hold a fretful realm in awe,
> And the kindly earth shall slumber, lapt in universal law.

For the Jews, the Messiah held such a promise. He was the one who would lead them to peace and security. The fact that Jesus did not show any signs of promoting or advocating the kind of perfect kingdom they expected caused the Jews to reject him.

Such dreams are not unique to Jews or Christians, however. Most societies have held some variation of that hope. Literature is full of such dreams and has inspired political movements which have captured the imagination of followers. Social and political groups such as the colonists who settled the Western Hemisphere, the socialist and communist movements, and the church have sought to establish perfect societies. Consider also the goals of the Holy Roman Empire, John Calvin's dream for the city of Geneva, or Joseph Smith's call for the perfect order of Zion.

In most cases when individuals or groups have set out to establish beneficent societies, the zeal with which they eventually tried to enforce their ideas of good has become the most diabolical and hellish of human endeavors. We need only remember the witch trials of Massachusetts, the Spanish Inquisition, or the repressive political climate of dictators to know the danger in the human disposition to displace God in guaranteeing peace. One of the ironies of human endeavor is that the consequences of the Fall have ensured that societies cannot save themselves. The attempts inevitably end in failure and devastating injustice because people's motivations are not pure and their wisdom is limited. The church knows this, but in desiring to achieve good it can easily forget that it must not assume the role of God. Essentially, it is the faith of the church that human ingenuity is not sufficient to bring about the ideal conditions for which people yearn. The church through the centuries has believed that the kingdom of God is the product of the New Being in Christ, a creation of divine and human initiative combined. The kingdom is the mission and work of God's sons and daughters. In spite of all this the church from time to time has lost the vision and tried to enforce its ideas on resisting people.

The following scripture is in harmony with the church's faith about the responsibilities of Christ's followers in bringing the kingdom into being:

I, the Lord, stretched out the heavens, and builded the earth as a very handy work; and all things therein are mine; and it is my purpose to provide for my saints, for all things are mine; but it must needs be done in mine own way.—Doctrine and Covenants 101:2d

Sometimes it is difficult for Christians to understand that their programs are not necessarily God's way. Paul, in writing to the Roman saints, related the temporal kingdom and the eternal nature together:

For the earnest expectation of the creature waiteth for the manifestation of the sons of God. . . . For we know that the whole creation groaneth and travaileth in pain together until now. And not only they, but ourselves also, which have the first fruits of the Spirit, even we ourselves groan within ourselves, waiting for the adoption, to wit, the redemption of our body.—Romans 8:19, 22, 23

Mixed Motives

In a practical way Christ's followers have always been challenged by the inner struggle to become new creatures in Christ. Through this struggle they attain freedom from those conditions described in the Fall and are remade in the image of Christ who is the first fruits of the new creation. For us, the struggle is both in yielding our own wills to God so that he can do in us what we cannot do for ourselves and in aggressively using our gifts in his service. The yielding to God and the valiant service are part and parcel of the divine call.

The early Christians were aware of this struggle of the soul. Paul wrote in eloquent terms about this inner conflict:

I find then that under the law, that when I would do good evil was present with me; for I delight in the law of God after the inward man. And now I see another law, even the commandment of Christ, and it is imprinted in my mind. But my members are warring against the law of my mind, and bringing me into captivity to the law of sin which is in my members. And if I subdue not the sin which is in me, but with the flesh serve the law of sin; O wretched man that I am! who shall deliver me from the body of this death? I thank God through Jesus Christ our Lord, then, that so with the mind I myself serve the law of God.—Romans 7:23-27

The life revealed in Jesus was honest. It speaks to us because it admits both the good and evil which we also experience. It is not some sedative to dull senses to the bitterness of reality nor a denial of our experience. Because of its honesty about life, the Christian faith confronts us with the supreme question: "What do we believe about the eventual victory of human self-interest as opposed to divine purpose?"

The interwoven strands of society which were evident in the climax of Christ's ministry were the symbols of the conflicting forces around us all the time. The Pharisees who tried to catch Jesus in some act which would justify his execution were no doubt convinced that his teachings threatened Judaism. His disregard for their religious customs and laws was undermining the basis of the Jewish faith. The fact is, of course, that the Pharisees' desires to maintain the purity of Judaism were also interlaced with motivations to protect their status and social position, their offended pride at being criticized by Jesus, and their arrogant feelings of superiority toward other people. These motivations of self-interest were so intermixed with their concern for maintaining the untainted faith of Judaism that they could not distinguish one from the other.

This is typical of the human predicament. Many personal commitments are clouded by less worthy or even unworthy desires to conform to the expectations of associates, personal desires to be important, and selfish interests which tempt people to be unjust to the minority in order to accomplish goals which appear to be of greater value to the majority. Humans have an amazing ability to rationalize their inner selfish desires; they convince themselves that achieving those desires is good even when it is evil.

In the human struggle to achieve good the injustice, cruelty, and ungodliness of those who think they are protecting the right often become a most satanic force. The forces opposed to Jesus are the supreme illustration of this fact. The Jewish leaders, the Roman soldiers, Pilate, and the little group of disciples were all motivated in some sense by their understanding of good, but they were also motivated by fear, greed, and vanity. The life of Jesus provoked the inherent conflict between the satanic and the godly which is in all human society. Because of this, the conflict was not between causes which could be identified as all evil as opposed to those which were all righteous. Seldom is conflict a result of issues which are so black and white.

In facing the problem of the human predicament with all its crosscurrents of motivation and human weakness, our sense of justice would condemn us. Only love is tough enough to hold in the face of our unworthiness. Here we begin in some measure to understand the grace of God who continues to identify with us even when we have fallen so short. We understand from the revelation in Christ that God, who created us and understands our predicament, continues to accept and love us even in our unworthiness. If this were not so none of us could be saved.

Because God accepts us we too can accept ourselves and others. We may have the courage to recognize our own failures and try again. We can accept each other and make allowances for human weakness, believing that God helps us when, with all our heart and strength, we want to be what he is calling us to be. We can face our weakness honestly without feeling rejected. This is the message of the cross and the Resurrection.

Does Evil Win?

The life of Jesus and the honesty with which it confronts the dilemmas of the human situation make the Christian faith cogent to all who believe. If the crucifixion were to be the end of the revelation found in Christ it would accurately illustrate the reality of the victory of human selfishness and cruelty over God. It would, in fact, say that when evil confronts good, evil wins; therefore, the satanic forces of this earth are ultimately the winners.

Many good people through the centuries have lived sacrificial lives. Some have been martyrs. If Christ is but one more of these, he holds out little hope to the human race. If he were truly the Son of God and his death on the cross the end, that would have been ever so much worse. It would have been the final evidence that even God does not have power to save his creation.

Precisely at this crucial point Christian faith bursts into radiance. When the tragedy of the cross seemed ultimate, the glory of Christ's resurrection startled the world with the new truth. Humankind has struggled from that day to this with the profound implication of that event. Suddenly what appeared to be cosmic defeat became cosmic victory. The future of the whole universe was at stake and God had won. Evil is not victorious. This does not imply that the victory was ever in doubt from the viewpoint of the eternal. But from the limited vision of those living in the temporal world this revelation of God's triumph was not clear until it was lived out in history by none other than Jesus Christ.

In Conclusion

The subject of the Resurrection is reserved for another chapter, but its significance is expanded in every dimension when seen in the light of the reality of the human complexity revealed in Jesus Christ. We humbly recognize that even our best human efforts to achieve the goals of the kingdom of God are saturated with our own self-interest, and that we easily take that which is intended to be righteous and turn it to evil. God who knows everything about his creation has by his amazing grace continued to identify with us as we are both good and bad. God loves us beyond human comprehension. He has paid the awesome price to live out in our midst the life which reveals what we are but reveals also, through the Resurrection, the amazing promise of what we shall become.

STUDY HELPS

1. How has the life of Jesus Christ prepared people for the harsh realities of the world of tragedy and confusion?
2. How does the house which stands on its firm foundation—as compared to one which topples from a foundation of sand—miss destruction but not the storm? The promise of God is eternal life, not unrealistic ease. Why do so many think that the evidence of God lies in the fact persons are often saved from the storm? How does the nature of your Christian commitment call you to suffer with God the contamination of the world?
3. The author is hard on those who feel they can escape reality either by time-filling activities or by assuming God's protection from all consequences. Do you agree or disagree? Why? How can you find a middle ground? What have you done in your life to offset the difficulties of living? How is it human to seek someone else (God, institutions, or other) to take responsibility? List some examples from your life of

ways you have given up responsibility or admitted responsibility for your own behavior.

4. What is the meaning of the kingdom of God? Some people are inclined to think of it as a form of government—democracy even. Do you agree? Why? Why not?
5. Why is a person's lifelong search for a peaceful social contract impossible unless all persons are obedient to the laws of God? You or other class members may like to research brief histories of some European and American schemes for establishing a utopia. How do these compare with the church's statements about Zion? How are they similar or different? Why?
6. Consider the plight of one who feels compelled to sin with good intent—to lie to save a dying person from distress, to steal to feed the sick and the weak. Are these cases of self-interest or unselfishness? Why? What does the life of Christ say about such behavior? When have you experienced this plight? How did you handle it? What would you now do differently?
7. Why do bad things happen to good people? What is the author's view on this question? What would you add, based on your life experiences?

CHAPTER 13

THE QUESTION OF BEING AND NONBEING

At times every person must grapple with the positive elements of life as opposed to death (nonbeing). People ask, "Is there life beyond death?" In its larger sense, sin, which is the source of evil, symbolizes the powers and structures of temporal existence which enslave and destroy being. God, who is the source of being, is at the same time engaged in the struggle to overcome evil and engender creative wholeness and health. In this vein, Jesus' mission is explained this way, "I am come that they might have life, and that they might have it more abundantly" (John 10:10). As God is the source of life, so Christ affirms life both through his revelation of its eternal dimensions and as the source of power to become the new being. Again John significantly declared, "As many as received him, to them gave he power to become the sons of God; only to them who believe on his name" (John 1:12).

Dealing with Death

Christian faith assures people that God participates with us in life, thus empowering us to successfully confront the destructive forces of sin and death. At times, however, all persons face situations when their faith is tested, and the nature—indeed, even the reality—of the continuation of being is doubted.

At some point we must anxiously contemplate death, questioning in what sense life continues beyond death.

We may also ask, "Is it possible that death is the total destruction of personal existence? Does one slip into nonbeing just as the rainbow vanishes when the clouds recede into the distance?" It will do no good to avoid the question or to try to force ourselves to believe without confronting the issue honestly.

Choosing Nonbeing

Many people's sense of personal worth is so shattered as to leave them without hope. Their center of existence is so vague as to leave them with no structure for integrating life. They are so ridden by guilt that they cannot bear the pain of the consequences of their acts. Such people may urgently want to achieve nonbeing. If we hold ourselves totally responsible for the tangled consequences of sin, unable to accept or forgive ourselves and unable to believe that God or other people will ever forgive us, life becomes unbearable and the possibility of escape from being is a relief.

In this situation the grace of God offers fresh hope and a new view of the value of life. We come to know that the Creator of the universe loves and accepts us and holds forth the opportunity, not for "old being" but for "new being."

Being Honest with Ourselves

Christian faith does not deny life's realities. We must each face honestly our situation, doubts, and thoughts of self-condemnation. Honesty, however, is a double-edged sword. Persons may be as dishonest in self-condemnation or in irrationally refusing to examine the soundness of the belief in immortality as in encouraging belief by "whistling in the dark."

The problem is aggravated by the fact that, just as it is impossible to prove that God is, it is impossible to prove that life continues beyond death. There are many reasons for believing both. When we are fully aware that there is no proof for or against the continuation of existence beyond death, and that we must consider possibilities rather than proof, we are impressed with the great weight of argument affirming immortality. Most of us find it more reasonable to believe in a continuing life than to deny it.

Looking at Death

In this struggle we must eventually ask, "What is the meaning of Christ's revelation for my personal existence?" We may believe in Christ as a great teacher, a good man, a prophecy of the kingdom, but this does not touch the question of continued existence. Since all people must deal with the universal problem of death, both for themselves and their loved ones, the question of Christ's personal revelation about immortality becomes crucial.

Life as Seen by Jesus

Everything about Jesus' ministry involved the continuing re-creation of life in the midst of the forces of sin and destruction. In his parable of the prodigal son, the father said, "For this my son was dead, and is alive again; he was lost, and is found" (Luke 15:24). Sin and death were correlated as twin expressions of the same destructive powers which oppose life. In relation to this Jesus said, "Fear not them who are able to kill the body, but are not able to kill the soul; but rather fear him who is able to destroy both soul and body in hell" (Matthew 10:25).

While in the common vernacular we speak of death as being that time when the vital organs of the body cease to function or when certain brain waves stop, when Jesus spoke of life his words held wider connotations of wholeness. Life for Jesus involved freedom and alignment with the divine purpose of creation. Christ was the center and source of that life: "I am the way, the truth, and the life" (John 14:6). In the story of Lazarus' death in the gospel of John, Jesus responds to Mary's grief by saying, "I am the resurrection, and the life; he that believeth in me, though he were dead, yet shall he live; and whosoever liveth and believeth in me shall never die" (John 11:25, 26). The Christian understanding of life and the continuing existence of being is more than physical or mental, and has dimensions which must be seen in relation to the divine intent for humankind. In the consideration of continued being we are confronted by the question of how our lives coincide with the eternal. Immortality has to do with the nature and quality of life, not merely its existence.

The Power of Christ's Life

The Christian faith does not deal in scientific proofs of continuing existence, and it has no rationale to show conclusively that humans are immortal. The Christian faith, rather, rests on the life of Christ which is lived out in our midst. Some aeronautical engineers once determined that by the laws of aerodynamics bumblebees ought not to be able to fly. Yet we note that they do fly.

In a similar fashion the Christian faith does not argue about the logic of immortality; Christ lives it out in our midst. While the dimensions of eternal life were resident within Jesus, those who experienced the impact of his person found their own lives being re-created. Just as the prodigal son was considered dead before returning to his father, so Mary Magdalene was overwhelmed by the powers of destruction before she met Jesus. He cast from her life those "devils" which were destroying her and she was restored. From her once frightful condition she became a woman of beauty and service. Of all those to whom Jesus might have appeared after his resurrection,

Mary Magdalene was among those to whom he first came.

When we consider such changes as those that came to Zacchaeus, to the blind man whose sight was restored, or to the common people who became his disciples, we know that Jesus brought healing, restoration, and wholeness wherever he touched lives.

The followers of Christ testify that his redirecting and restoring power has continued to be experienced in their midst. Jesus is the living Christ. We are the beneficiaries of the forgiving, lifting, restorative power of the Holy Spirit which has introduced healing and new life into our weary existence. When thinking of what we might have been we know that the power of Christ has lifted us from death unto life.

The Power of the Resurrection

The final dramatic events in the physical life of Jesus revealed the implications of the restorative principle in the death and resurrection. Sin-ridden persons were freed and made righteous, the sick and impotent were healed, even the dead restored to life; but these remained mortal beings. It was quite a different reality when, after his ignominious suffering and death on the cross, the risen and immortal Lord appeared in the midst of his disciples. This was no argument about immortality and the possibility of continuing life, no theories, just the compelling evidence. At first this seemed incomprehensible. Peter and John ran to the empty tomb, unable to fathom the meaning of what they had heard (John 20:2-9).

Luke recorded that as the disciples were gathered discussing the strange news, Jesus appeared in their midst and spoke to them:

> But they were terrified and affrighted, and supposed that they had seen a spirit. And he said unto them, Why are you troubled, and why

do thoughts arise in your hearts? Behold my hands and my feet, that it is I, myself. Handle me, and see; for a spirit hath not flesh and bones, as you see me have. When he had thus spoken, he showed them his hands and feet.—Luke 24:36-39

Because they still did not understand, Jesus asked for food and when they gave him a piece of broiled fish and a honeycomb, he ate before them. Jesus' resurrection was such an unexpected event that the Gospel of John indicates Thomas could not accept the credibility of the reports until confronted by the risen Lord and shown the evidences of his crucifixion. Then, as so often happens, not argument but the overwhelming confrontation with the Lord himself made Thomas confess, "My Lord and my God."

In the midst of this, the disciples must all have begun to recall Christ's earlier teachings:

In my Father's house are many mansions; if it were not so, I would have told you. I go to prepare a place for you. And when I go, I will prepare a place for you, and come again, and receive you unto myself; that where I am, ye may be also.—John 14:2, 3

In this spirit and with these understandings, it appears that the early Christians were relatively unafraid of death or the persecutions which so soon followed Christ's ascension.

The testimony of the scriptures is very moving. We can hardly accept Christ as the Son of God without accepting the testimony of his resurrection and what it means for our own immortality. Our self-understanding is thereby transformed.

Avoid Assuming Too Much

We ought to carefully avoid drawing conclusions that the scriptures do not warrant. While the testimonies of Christ's physical appearance after his death are clear, there were dimensions of his resurrected body in these accounts that were not common to mortality. For instance, he appeared and disappeared in ways which were not typical of human mortality. Although Jesus showed his hands and feet as evidence of his identity, many who knew him well seemed not to recognize the resurrected Christ. In fact, it appears that they recognized him by the spirit of his presence rather than by his physical form. That spiritual presence continued to be experienced among them after his ascension. They referred to this as "the mind of Christ" or the "Holy Ghost."

Recognizing then the difficulty of absolutely identifying in any minute detail the characteristics of Christ's resurrected body, the early Christians were content to affirm:

> Beloved, now we are the sons of God, and it doth not yet appear what we shall be; but we know that, when he shall appear, we shall be like him; for we shall see him as he is. And every man that hath this hope in him purifieth himself, even as he is pure.—I John 3:2, 3

Their faith was in the general experience of the Resurrection; it did not require detailed descriptions. The Resurrection gave assurance that nothing any people or governments could do to them could take from them the victory they had been guaranteed in Christ. This removed their fear and sent them forth as witnesses to the new life they had found in Christ.

In Conclusion

The question of personal being and the threat of nonbeing is a universal concern. Most world religions deal with this question in some fashion. For Christians, however, the meaning of existence and the assurance of immortality are revealed in the life, death, and resurrection of the Lord Jesus Christ. It is not couched in an argument but in a life. This amazing revelation of life's continuing dimensions has transformed the understanding of persons about themselves, their loved ones, and all humanity. It lifts our understanding of life from the immediate to the eternal.

STUDY HELPS

1. The author states that sin is the source of all evil. Many persons would suggest that the explanation lies the other way around. From your reading thus far, explain why you feel the author has made this statement. Do you agree or disagree? Why?
2. Why is it so difficult for most persons, even devout Christians who believe in a life after death, to face their own deaths? Consider the paradox of life versus eternal life. What is the appeal of each to you? Why?
3. What is the meaning of the idea of nonbeing? What about it is most appealing? What is most fearful? The whole idea suggests that things which are can cease to be. How is this possible? Why? Why not?
4. Jesus' use of the term *life* was more than casual. How did he use the term? How does this use relate to the chapters dealing with a person's wholeness? How did Jesus use *death* and *life*?
5. How is the idea of being restored related or not related to being resurrected? How do these have vastly different understandings? In what ways are they alike? How do people confuse them in their worship and understanding? How are these used in the scriptures? In what ways may they be confused? How have you used these terms? What would you change after reading this idea?
6. Early Christians felt Jesus would be returning almost immediately. His assurance, "I will prepare a place for you, and come again, and receive you unto myself; that where I am ye may be also," suggests a

return. Some Christians believe this to be a physical return while others believe this is the promise of a Comforter. With which view do you agree? Why? How was the early Latter Day Saint view similar to that of the early Christian disciples?

7. The Resurrection is often seen as "the revelation of being as opposed to nonbeing." What are several meanings which resurrection has for the Christian? Why? What is your belief about the Resurrection? How is it similar or different from the author's? Do you agree with the author's statement, "We can hardly accept Christ as the Son of God without accepting the testimony of his resurrection and what it means for our own immortality" (page 136)? Why or why not?

CHAPTER

THE WONDER OF THE RESURRECTION

Many people find the primary meaning of the Resurrection in its revelation of being, as opposed to nonbeing. The Apostle Paul wrote to the Corinthian saints saying:

> When this corruptible shall have put on incorruption, and this mortal shall have put on immortality, then shall be brought to pass the saying that is written, Death is swallowed up in victory. O death, where is thy sting? O grave, where is thy victory?—I Corinthians 15:54, 55

Christians sing hallelujahs and songs of amazed joy. The Easter period has become a time for celebrating new life.

Deeper Meanings of the Resurrection

While Christians never lose the joy and wonder of the personal implications in Christ's resurrection, the followers of Christ have through the centuries recognized a far wider and deeper meaning. The Resurrection is the culminating evidence that God is Creator, Ruler, and King of the universe.

We affirm that God is the creator and sustainer of the temporal universe. God is as he is, not because people made him that way or because the influence of the temporal world shaped him to be the kind of God he is. We are conditioned by the influence of environment to be as we are. God is not influenced by the environment; he is unconditioned. Therefore, he is what he is because he is God. We have not made God; he has made us.

All time and space were created by God. He is the source and author of all existence. So-called natural law is the expression of God's will. Because God is trustworthy and consistent the laws of the universe are dependable, but they are subject to his will and purpose and obedient to his command. God's laws are subject to him—not vice versa.

God is the source of all power and energy. Although we as created beings may in our limited way exercise power and control energy, in the ultimate sense all power and energy originate from God. We only exercise and control that power which is God's as he allows us to do so.

God is the source and sustainer of all life. He grants life and in the end all life is dependent on him.

God is king because he is the owner of all things. The ownership which people exercise is always subject to God, and it is temporary. Even those who count themselves rich and powerful in material things can hope to exercise their limited control for only a few short years before they must relinquish everything to God. Our bodies belong to God and we must yield them back to God. All that we have is given back to God at the time of physical death. While we live we exercise a stewardship over life.

New Meaning to God

The preceding statements are not new. Even before Christ came the human race had some knowledge of God and his nature. Nevertheless, the revelation which came in the life of Jesus was a startling and cogent expression of God's divine nature. Those who knew Christ understood God in dimensions they had not known before.

The prophets had testified of God as creator, and in the Psalms and closing chapters of the book of Job the fact of God's majestic creatorship was affirmed. Yet it was Jesus who made the simple declaration of God as creator powerfully clear. When he taught he did so as one "having authority."

He spoke of God as creator and proclaimed him to be everyone's Father. In this affirmation people understood God to be not an impersonal or mechanical creator but a loving parent. This gave meaning to the early declaration that God created humanity in his own image: "And I, God, created man in mine own image, in the image of mine Only Begotten created I him; male and female created I them" (Genesis 1:29). This raised people's understanding of the level of human relationship with the Divine. The concept was not only personal; it clearly characterized the nature of God as one of amazing love. The relationship of God to each person could never again be seen as it had been before Jesus' existence.

The Meaning of the Miracles

Since the days Jesus walked the roads of Galilee, people have tried to explain his miracles. While he always avoided performing miracles to impress people or win their allegiance, it is clear that those forces which are called natural law responded to his will. He rebuked the winds and the tempestuous sea, and they responded to his command (Matthew 8:24-27). He healed the sick and gave life to the dead. He fed the multitude from five loaves and two fishes (Matthew 14:15-18). He cursed the unfruitful fig tree and it died (Matthew 21:17). We need not multiply the illustrations of the control of Jesus over the temporal world, but we must comprehend these acts for what they were. They were not the work of some magician or man who was merely wiser than his companions. Jesus was making it crystal clear that God, the creator of the temporal universe, directs his creation.

This expression of God's power and will over the universe was the final assurance that human and cosmic events are within God's control. While he grants the human exercise of agency, in the ultimate sense God is the source of all power and is able to keep that which is his. In that same sense we trust ourselves into God's care, knowing he is able ultimately to keep us even in death.

Jesus' Revelation of God as Giver of Life

Jesus revealed God's power to give and preserve life, both through healing the body and mind and through raising those who were dead. In this he was not merely expressing his compassion for those who suffered or grieved for a loved one. Each miracle was an occasion to show that God is the author and giver of life.

Resurrection as Validation of the Sonship of Jesus

Any thoughtful study of the birth and life of Jesus points both to the omnipotent power of God and to the tremendous potential invested in persons. All the evidences portrayed in the life and ministry of Jesus would have fallen short, however, had there been no resurrection.

The final dramatic week was amazing. During that week the disciples shared the exultation of Jesus' ride into Jerusalem, the sobering experience of the Last Supper, the pain of Gethsemane, the trial, and finally the crucifixion. Then Jesus was buried. For the disciples it seemed as if their dream was ended. Perhaps the two disciples on the road to Emmaus expressed the great disappointment best: "The chief priests and our rulers delivered him to be condemned to death, and have crucified him. But we trusted that it had been he who should have redeemed Israel" (Luke 24:19, 20). To them the cause appeared to be lost. Jesus was dead. The disciples were ready to go back to their fishing nets or other pursuits.

The rest of the world would have taken little note of all that Jesus had done and said if his life had ended on the cross. The resurrection transformed all of Jesus' past life and all of past history. It was the startling validation that he was the Son of God. It was the sudden confirmation that what Jesus had been and said in their midst was true in ways the disciples had never dreamed possible. Not only was Jesus the Son of God but also their understanding of God took on new meaning and vitality. God was the source of life. Death was not supreme or final. God was the victor. The whole world was seen in a different light, as if it had become a new world.

Resurrection as Validation of the Omnipotence of God

The Resurrection was the validation that the things which had been said about God's creative, omnipotent, unconditional power and love were true. Jesus' disciples had not dared to believe before, but now they were assured, and with that assurance they were willing to trust their lives and futures to the care of God. They did not demand to know the future. It was sufficient to know that their future was in the hands of God whose love they had experienced in Jesus and whose omnipotent power was sufficient for their every need.

Resurrection as Inspiration for Witnessing

The change in the lives of Jesus' followers was so significant and the joy so pervasive that the early saints came to feel that the greatest thing they could do was to introduce and win others to the faith which had transformed them. This urgent desire is symbolized in the request that John made to tarry until Jesus should come again (John 21:22) and in the desire of the three Nephite disciples to remain to win others to Christ (III Nephi 13:15-22). It is seen in the vital witness that went forth from the little band of Christ's followers which composed the early church.

Resurrection as Guarantee of Victory

Although the Christian experience still had to await the day of Pentecost, the resurrection of Christ was a primary event in establishing the church and transforming the disciples of Jesus. In their minds and hearts they knew that from that day forward the victory was guaranteed by God. They could therefore say with the Apostle Paul, "Thanks be unto God for his unspeakable gift" (II Corinthians 9:15). No words could adequately express the meaning that now pervaded the world because of the Resurrection.

In Conclusion

The Resurrection was a revelation of the continuing personal being of each one who believed in Jesus Christ, the Son of God. That comprehension of eternal life in immortality had a profound effect on all who witnessed the risen Lord. It changed their understanding of themselves and of their relation to God and the universe. This assurance—that each person like Jesus shall participate in the Resurrection—has made the celebration of Easter stand alongside Christmas as the two most significant Christian days of celebration. Easter is a day of joy and triumph.

In spite of the great significance of the Resurrection for each person's continuing existence beyond death, its greatest significance was in its validation of the creative, omnipotent, loving nature of God. The Jews had accepted God but never before had they understood him to be the majestic, powerful, compassionate Father that Jesus revealed. God was the giver and source of existence. All things were subject to him. Because of his revealed love for each person, those who believed loved him with an intensity and quality beyond the love people had previously known.

God was the giver of life and the controller of history. Christ's followers were now assured that his purposes would be fulfilled. The victory was guaranteed in him. While the descriptions of the future were incomplete and the disciples could not draw conclusions about what God would do, they were assured that his love for them was so unconditional and his power to fulfill his purposes so all-inclusive that they could put their trust in him. They knew he would do so much more than they had yet conceived; therefore, they were willing to give their lives freely to him in loving confidence. The amazing events of the Resurrection so far surpassed anything that they had ever dreamed possible that they chose no longer to limit the future to their own human concepts. It was sufficient to know God and trust him through faith in the Lord Jesus Christ.

STUDY HELPS

1. How are miracles by God a disruption of natural law? In what ways may they be expressions of natural laws yet unknown? How are miracles consistent with the author's view of the dependability of the "laws of the universe"? Why? Why not?
2. God is seen as creator, the source of all power and energy. What then is meant by the scripture, "Man was also in the beginning with God. Intelligence, or

the light of truth, was not created or made, neither indeed can be" (Doctrine and Covenants 90:5a)? How are these compatible? Incompatible?

3. What is the meaning of the word *law?* How does the author view the law? How does the author's view differ from yours? How are they the same?
4. The author states that "the Resurrection validated the sonship of Jesus." What is the meaning of this statement? Why was the resurrection of Jesus necessary as the culmination of his earthly ministry?
5. Consider the preceding question in the light of Apostle Paul's statement, "Thanks be unto God for his unspeakable gift" (II Corinthians 9:15). How have you thanked God for the gift of his Son?
6. Read chapter 17 of *Exploring the Faith* for further clarification of these topics. You may like to share your finding with a class or friend. Suggest how this chapter relates to the author's views.
7. Look at page 15 of *Exploring the Faith* and read paragraph 17. How are disciples required to respond to Jesus Christ? What may be some indications that a person's soul has been quickened and transformed? When is this something people can bring about? How are they totally dependent on God's grace? Why? How have you responded to Jesus Christ? Share an experience in which you felt quickened and transformed.
8. The author says that "God is not influenced by the environment." Do you agree or disagree? Under what circumstances might God be influenced by human action? In what situations might God be subject to his own laws?

CHAPTER

THE EXPERIENCE OF THE HOLY SPIRIT

The power of the ministry of Jesus is a striking fact. From the initial impact on Andrew who, after listening to Jesus, immediately went in search of his brother Simon Peter (John 1:37-42), to the astonished woman of Samaria who was confronted by Jesus while drawing water from a well (John 4:9-31), the power of Jesus profoundly affected people. There was about him a spirit which drew people. His followers had varying expectations regarding his work, but they all wanted to be with Jesus. He was welcome in their homes, sought in times of sickness, and followed by multitudes who were hungry for the words of life which he spoke.

It is not surprising then that those closest to Jesus were incredulous when he spoke of leaving them. They did not want him to go and they could not understand how his early death could fit into their anticipations for his mission. Even more unthinkable was his somber pronouncement to the Twelve that one of them would betray him (Luke 22:21-23).

Preparation for Departure

In such a context of apprehension and confusion, the Gospel of John tells of Jesus speaking to his disciples about his departure, "I tell you the truth; It is expedient for you that I go away; for if I go not away, the Comforter will not come unto you; but if I depart, I will send him unto you" (John 16:7).

The idea and experience of the Holy Spirit was not

new to the disciples. The Hebrew writings bore witness to the illuminating power of the Holy Spirit; some passages were the product of prophets who wrote under the influence of the Holy Spirit. It appears, however, that the reference of Jesus to the Comforter carried a dimension which the disciples did not comprehend. Jesus is recorded saying that the Comforter would "reprove the world of sin, and of righteousness, and of judgment" (John 16:8), "He will guide you into all truth . . . and he will show you things to come" (John 16:13), and "He shall glorify me; for he shall receive of mine, and shall show it unto you" (John 16:14). In other experiences they were to learn that the Holy Spirit brought understanding, strength, and peace. The Holy Spirit would be a constant reminder to them of the things Jesus had said and done in their presence.

In the midst of their sorrow and apprehension about this announcement of imminent death Jesus said, "In the world ye shall have tribulation; but be of good cheer; I have overcome the world" (John 16:33). It was not his purpose to burden his followers but to prepare them for the week which was so soon to follow. That week left the disciples unready for the future even though Jesus had done so much to prepare them. True it was that the Resurrection had changed everything, yet Jesus cautioned them in those few days before his ascension not to move too quickly into the mission he had called them to undertake. Matthew ends his gospel with the "great commission":

> Go ye therefore, and teach all nations, baptizing them in the name of the Father, and of the Son, and of the Holy Ghost; teaching them to observe all things whatsoever I have commanded you; and, lo, I am with you always, unto the end of the world.—Matthew 28:18, 19

In Luke, however, the disciples are advised to wait a little while, "And, behold, I send the promise of my Father upon you; but tarry ye in the city of Jerusalem, until ye be endued with power from on high" (Luke 24:48). No doubt there was need for them to sort through the amazing array of experience that had so recently occurred to them and to reorient their lives to the new meanings that had grasped them. There was imperative need for the unfathomed experience of the Comforter.

Recognized by His Spirit

Even in their contacts with Christ after the resurrection his followers recognized him more by the familiar spirit of his presence than by a physical form. In one account in the gospel of John, he showed the nail prints in his hands and feet to convince his followers that he was indeed Jesus Christ, but even so the disciples on the way to Emmaus, after walking, talking, and dining with him, did not recognize Christ until he blessed the food and was taken out of their sight (Luke 24:29, 30). While the gospel of Luke states that their eyes "were holden" (Luke 24:15), it is significant that when they realized Jesus had been their companion, "They said one to another, Did not our hearts burn within us, while he talked with us by the way, and while he opened to us the scriptures?" (Luke 24:31). This spirit of his presence identified him most surely. In like manner he was not recognized by Mary when he first appeared to her in the garden until he spoke her name (John 20:16). The disciples who had fished unsuccessfully all night did not recognize Christ standing on the shore until he caused their nets to be so filled that they could not draw in the fishes (John 21:6).

While the resurrected Lord was with the disciples in physical being, even in those few days before the ascension, they were being prepared to associate his presence with the spirit of Christ more than with a physical form.

Day of Pentecost Experience

When on the day of Pentecost the Comforter came in mighty power, the people who observed were astonished and the believers were transformed. Peter preached with such power that many who heard were convinced that his affirmation was true. They cried out, "Men and brethren, what shall we do?" (Acts 2:37). Early Christian writers told that about three thousand were baptized that day (Acts 2:41).

The disciples of Jesus clearly related the Comforter to his continuing presence. Although he was gone, there was a deeper sense in which he was ever present in their midst. Jesus was no longer limited by location or physical barriers. He was the abiding Comforter. He was with them in ministry, in perfecting the young church, in times of persecution, and in prison. They thought of him as the ever-present Christ, not living in some distant heavenly realm but everywhere among and within them by his presence.

In witnessing it was as if their minds were opened; Christ gave them thoughts and words to convince those searching for truth and to confound the enemies of the church. When they prayed, he was within, guiding their thoughts to God who was outside them. It was an unexplainable experience which they related to Christ's continuing presence.

The early disciples expected Christ's imminent return in body, but in the interim Christ was with them in spirit. That spirit was experienced so intimately that the scriptural writers appear to use synonymously such terms as "Comforter," "Holy Ghost," "Spirit of God," "Holy Spirit," "Spirit of Jesus Christ," or the "mind of Christ." They recognized that this spirit was a way by which they experienced God in the same essential qualities of personhood that they had known in Christ.

Testimony of the Holy Spirit

The early church came to understand that the most important function of the Holy Spirit was to witness to the inner person that Jesus is the Christ with all that such a conviction means for transforming life. This understanding led the Apostle Paul to say, "Wherefore I give you to understand, that no man speaking by the Spirit of God calleth Jesus accursed; and that no man can say that Jesus is the Lord, but by the Holy Ghost" (I Corinthians 12:3). In the centuries that followed, this function of the Holy Spirit stood out as preeminent. Some have emphasized the healing power of the Holy Spirit as it has brought physical or mental health to the sick; others have looked to the Holy Spirit as the source of light and intelligence. Some have found comfort and assurance in the ministry of the Holy Spirit in times of grief, and some have been strengthened to face life and death through the Holy Spirit. All of these, however, are subordinate to, and, in essential ways, dependent on, the testimony that Jesus is the living Christ.

Creation of a New Spirit

Chief among the implications of conversion to Christ is the understanding that the work of Christ in people is to reconcile us to each other and to God. The Holy Spirit is that reconciling power which bears witness of Christ and works within to transform us into reconciled sons and daughters of God. This could not be done by law. This is accomplished only by the power to re-create a new spirit within the person. The Old Testament prophets had foretold such a transformation:

> A new heart also will I give you, and a new spirit will I put within you; and I will take away the stony heart out of your flesh, and I will give you a heart of flesh. And I will put my Spirit within you, and cause you to walk in my statutes, and ye shall keep my judgments and do them. And ye shall dwell in the land that I gave to your

fathers; and ye shall be my people, and I will be your God.—Ezekiel 36:26-28

While it is not helpful here to identify a time or event in which Ezekiel's prophecy was fulfilled, it foreshadows the kind of spiritual rebirth the early saints experienced. Paul could write, "Therefore if any man live in Christ, he is a new creature; old things are passed away; behold, all things are become new" (II Corinthians 5:17).

Confirmation of Ministry

In the early church the Holy Spirit powerfully accompanied the preaching and witnessing of the followers of Christ so that the disciples could say, "For our gospel came not unto you in word only, but also in power, and in the Holy Ghost, and in much assurance" (I Thessalonians 1:5). The Holy Spirit was recognized not only as the power which convicted persons to believe in Christ, but also the sign that God was confirming his intention that those converted be accepted into the church.

This was a basic issue among the early Christians and was at the heart of Peter and Paul's disagreement. Those members coming out of Palestinian Judaism could hardly accept the fact that God would receive non-Jews who had not complied with the Jewish law and rites.

Peter's experience in Joppa helped convince him and prepare him for ministry to the Gentiles. In a vision he saw the heavens opened and a sheet let down filled with food which the Jews considered unclean. While he was contemplating what the vision meant and why the voice had said, "What God hath cleansed, that call not thou common" (Acts 10:15), the servants of a non-Jewish centurion came to ask Peter to come and explain to them the meaning of God's instruction. When Peter responded he found that "the Holy Ghost fell on all them which heard the word." Peter, seeing this, could only say, "Can any man forbid water, that these should not be baptized, which have received the Holy Ghost as well as we?" (Acts 10:44-47).

For the traditional members of the church coming out of Judaism, this was unthinkable. Although the conflict in the minds of the Palestinian Jews was not easily resolved, Paul stood firm for the principle that the church should be inclusive rather than another sect of Judaism. The conclusive evidence of the broader outreach of the church, however, was the fact that God was extending the gift of the Holy Spirit to these Gentiles. The author of Acts narrates Peter's later argument to the church:

> As I began to speak, the Holy Ghost fell on them, as on us at the beginning. Then remembered I the word of the Lord, how that he said, John indeed baptized with water; but ye shall be baptized with the Holy Ghost. Forasmuch then as God gave them the like gift as he did unto us, who believed on the Lord Jesus Christ, what was I, that I could withstand God?—Acts 11:15-17

The Laying On of Hands

While the early church did accept the principle that the Holy Spirit was given as God willed, it was regarded as a power imparted from person to person by the laying on of hands (Acts 8:14-17). Largely, however, the testimony of the Holy Spirit in the early church is not doctrinal in nature; it is a record of experiences. When the early Christians experienced the marvelous power of the Holy Spirit they were grateful for the gift and amazed at the changes God wrought in them through his power. They did not demand a systematic doctrine of the Holy Spirit. This gift resulted not in argument but in testimony. They said to the unbelieving, "Come and see."

In Conclusion

While the day of Pentecost was marked by spectacular and dramatic evidences of the power of the Holy

Spirit, the longtime experience of the abiding presence of the Spirit of Christ, or the Holy Ghost, was more intimate and personal. It was recognized as that same presence they had felt in Christ, sometimes called the mind of Christ.

After Pentecost the Holy Spirit was not limited in time or location. The followers of Christ experienced the Spirit everywhere. The Comforter could be in all the world and with every person at the same moment—the living, vibrant Christ to all who believed.

The Holy Spirit enlightened the minds and guided the thoughts of Christ's followers. The Holy Spirit strengthened the saints and took away fear, but it also filled them with love and reconciled them to God and each other. It even gave them compassion for their enemies. In the same spirit with which Jesus had prayed for forgiveness for the soldiers who crucified him, so Stephen also cried in his dying moments for those who were stoning him, saying, "Lord, lay not this sin to their charge" (Acts 7:60).

The Holy Spirit reminded Christians of the things Jesus had taught and done before his ascension, but it brought deeper meaning and wider application to those same events. The early saints found the promise in John happening in their lives, "I have yet many things to say unto you, but ye cannot bear them now. Howbeit when he, the Spirit of truth, is come, he will guide you into all truth" (John 16:12, 13).

Most of all the Holy Spirit was the power which penetrated the hearts of people to convince them that Jesus was and is the Christ. The Holy Ghost worked within their hearts, transforming them into spiritually begotten sons and daughters of God.

That Spirit of the living Christ has been the ever-present testimony accompanying the witness of the church through the centuries. The church has experienced and validated the promise of Christ:

> Abide in me, and I in you. As the branch cannot bear fruit of itself, except it abide in the vine, no more can ye, except ye abide in me. I am the vine, ye are the branches. He that abideth in me, and I in him, the same bringeth forth much fruit; for without me ye can do nothing.—John 15:4, 5

This experience is universal. The church is the church of Jesus Christ when it is led by his Spirit into his mission.

STUDY HELPS

1. What may have motivated Judas to betray Jesus?
2. Why did Jesus make no apparent effort either to stop Judas or to talk with him about it? Was the betrayal necessary? Why? How was it determined by God? How may Judas have been unjustly criticized? What do your answers suggest about the experience of one who betrays the Master?
3. What is the definition of *comforter?* How is the author's view similar or different from that found in the dictionary?
4. List the possible reasons why the disciples did not recognize Christ after the Resurrection? What made recognition possible when it did come? How do you see Christ in the people and events around you?
5. Read pages 200 to 205 in *Exploring the Faith.* You or another student may like to read this in advance and then share only the highlights. What does it say concerning the Holy Spirit? How is the Comforter God's revelation to persons?
6. What role did the Holy Spirit have regarding the ministry of Jesus and the disciples? How does this view of the Holy Spirit compare to your own perspective? The Spirit confirms in a manner different in meaning and intensity. In what scripture account

did the Spirit minister to Christ? His disciples?

7. How was the early Christian church inclusive? Today's church has been exclusive. How does this limit the outreach of the Saints to people with special needs? How is this exclusiveness in violation of Christ's teachings? What are some evidences of a growing inclusiveness? What do you do to be inclusive? Share with another person or the class an experience when God's Spirit helped you reach out to another person.

CHAPTER 16

AN EMBARRASSMENT TO THE CHURCH

The twin experiences of the Resurrection and the day of Pentecost launched the church and sent forth the little band of disciples afire with the witness of Jesus Christ. They told the story of Christ crucified, risen from the tomb, and alive in the hearts and minds of his followers everywhere. It was a powerful story. Even the unbelievers recognized that such men as Peter and John were now different. "They marveled; and they took knowledge of them, that they had been with Jesus" (Acts 4:13).

The experience of the church with the Holy Spirit was soon accompanied by problems. The problems were old but probably not anticipated by the disciples. The difficulty centered in the ever-present conflict between magic and genuine spiritual expression.

Magic and Spiritual Experience

Magic is centered in the supposition that persons can learn to control and use unknown natural or supernatural forces to serve their personal wishes. The idea of magic is often attributed to divine intervention in the Old Testament scriptures, but is in no way limited to the scriptural narrative. Most societies have had their oracles and wonder-workers. Even in today's modern societies there are those who want to believe in the power of astrology or extrasensory manipulation.

This problem is similar to the worship of idols. An

idol is an image or thing which can be owned or manipulated by people in the belief that it can bring good fortune in time of famine, disease, war, or other evils over which persons feel they have no control. The idol is thought to have supernatural powers and to be subject to the persons who own or worship it. Idols give people a feeling of safety and that they have no need for God. Modern societies have made idols of science and technology, wealth, government, and military superiority.

In opposition to magic, genuine spiritual experience puts God at the center. It does not cause persons to expect or desire the power of the universe to revolve around them. Persons come to understand that they want not their will but God's will. They do not seek to coerce God into doing their bidding but to learn God's will and yield their lives to it. Sometimes this is difficult. In the Garden of Gethsemane Jesus did not find it easy to yield to the will of God and say, "Father, if thou be willing, remove this cup from me; nevertheless not my will, but thine be done" (Luke 22:42). This was the model for Christ's followers, that Christians want to become identified with God's purposes rather than to impose their purposes on God.

Early Christians and the Problem

The struggle between the natural desires of persons to be God, with the universe revolving around them, and valid spiritual experience in which persons choose God's purposes and yield their lives to him is ever present. The early church immediately found this misunderstanding of the Holy Spirit emerging. When Peter and John went to the city of Samaria to confirm those who had been newly baptized through the laying on of hands, the event was eagerly witnessed. Simon, who had formerly bewitched the people with sorcery, now tried to buy the power to grant the Holy Ghost:

When Simon saw that through laying on of the apostles' hands the Holy Ghost was given, he offered them money, saying, Give me also this power, that on whomsoever I lay hands, he may receive the Holy Ghost. But Peter said unto him, Thy money perish with thee, because thou hast thought that the gift of God may be purchased with money. Thou hast neither part nor lot in this matter; for thy heart is not right in the sight of God.—Acts 8:18-21

Simon was a magician, not a spiritual minister.

Unfortunately for the early church, all the misunderstandings and spurious activities attributed to the Holy Spirit were not as easily discerned as was Simon's crass request. The human desire for selfish gain from the Holy Spirit is much more insidious and difficult to discern. Persons within the church who wanted power or popular acclaim often wrote or spoke things they attributed to the Holy Ghost. Perhaps in their intense desire many even believed themselves that their thoughts were approved by the Holy Spirit. These writings were sometimes circulated among the churches as inspired instruction. It was a common practice for lesser known persons to write what they wanted the church to accept and list the authorship as some well-known church leader.

Confrontation with Spurious Gifts

The consequence of false teachings is readily discerned in such letters as Paul's instruction to the churches of Galatia:

I marvel that ye are so soon removed from him that called you into the grace of Christ unto another gospel; which is not another; but there be some that trouble you, and would pervert the gospel of Christ. But though we, or an angel from heaven, preach any other gospel unto you than that which we have preached unto you, let him be accursed.—Galatians 1:6-8

While the active participation of the Holy Spirit had been an essential element in establishing the church, the disposition of persons to claim the authority of the Holy

Spirit for their actions and writings was a great threat. Some of this activity was personally generated and for personal gain. It was a constant embarrassment to the church. Keeping the spurious components of magic from creeping into the church and confusing the saints was an ever-present concern. As we read the New Testament, we get the impression that both Paul and John were very active in trying to keep a healthy spiritual life in the church. They stood against the false manifestations attributed to the Holy Spirit.

Protection Through Scriptures

The maturing church inevitably found ways to protect itself from the confusion and embarrassment of this uncontrolled claim to spiritual authority. Church leaders began to identify certain writings which they considered to be genuinely inspired by the Holy Spirit and the testimony of those who were eyewitnesses to or actually involved in the ministry of Christ and the fledgling church. This was a long process. There were differences of opinion about the validity of certain writings. Eventually, however, the most widely accepted agreement was reached by the Council of Trent (1545-1563). Of course some variation exists in the books accepted by various Christian groups as scripture. In general, however, common agreement is found on the writings accepted as New Testament scripture.

Church leaders involved in the selection process were not engaged in judging all writings to determine whether or not each was inspired. Rather they set out to select a core of inspired and accurate writings which they considered to contain the essential testimony and teachings necessary to lead people to salvation. Those church leaders would have thought that there may be many inspired and semi-inspired writings not included in the Bible, but the Bible includes all that is necessary for people to know and follow to be saved. If people follow the Bible they will not be led away into false doctrine.

Church Structure and Policy Regarding the Holy Spirit

The church began to limit the expression of the Holy Spirit in an attempt to weed out that which was false. The church (Roman Catholic at this time) not only accepted scripture as the official repository of the Holy Spirit's expression, but began to designate ways in which it would accept utterances of the Holy Spirit. Gregory the Great maintained that the councils composing the leadership of the church were guided by the Holy Spirit and should be so recognized. In 1870 a Vatican Council declared "a divinely revealed dogma" that "when the Roman Pontiff speaks *ex cathedra* . . . he possess that power of infallibility with which the Divine Redeemer willed that His Church should be furnished in defining doctrine on faith or morals." With this final act it corralled the expressions of the Holy Spirit which it would officially accept. Catholics as well as other Christians feel there is some irony in the fact that the church which attributes its origin to the creative action of the Holy Spirit should make that Holy Spirit a prisoner of the church. In this century there has been a rebirth of the charismatic expression in many Christian churches, but these expressions have not been given the status of scripture.

Protestants and the Holy Spirit

The same ferment out of which the Council of Trent reached its decision and effectively closed the canon of scripture also accompanied the Protestant Reformation. While one might have expected the Protestant revolt to reclaim the freedom and spontaneity of the Holy Spirit, such leaders as Luther and Calvin tended to shy away from the problems this would create. In general, classic Protestantism took the position that the scriptures were the written word from the Holy Spirit. It was therefore the function of the Holy Spirit to witness to the reader or hearer of the word the truth of it. The Protestant movement which had rejected the authority of the pope and the Roman church vested that authority in the Bible. While the Holy Spirit was believed to be active in the hearts of the members of the church, its focus was confined within the records of the past as they were contained in the scriptures.

The Latter Day Saint Movement

When Joseph Smith experienced the active movement of the Holy Spirit in his life and, naïve lad that he was, went to the clergy for help in interpreting his spiritual experiences, he was rebuffed. This is not surprising. The mentors of the Christian world denied the validity of such spiritual manifestations.

The consequences of this conflict which brought such opposition to the early Latter Day Saint church need not be discussed here. Yet it is important that one of the major characteristics of the Latter Day Saint movement was its belief in, and active experience with, the Holy Spirit. Latter Day Saints saw themselves as experiencing a restoration of the vital creative action of the Holy Spirit so cogently described in the book of Acts. Those involved in the Latter Day Saint movement were convinced that God was immediately at hand, and they were set on fire with the desire to witness to others about the marvelous things that had happened.

Unfortunately the same prostitution of the Holy Spirit that had reared its head among the early Christians embarrassed the fledgling Latter Day Saint movement. Shortly after the church was founded, a man by the name of Hiram Page claimed to have received "revelations" through the use of a stone. He brought an element of confusion and divisiveness to the church. Doctrine and Covenants 27 addresses this problem. It places some restraints and outlines the order for receiving and accepting expressions of the Holy Spirit by the church.

Although the Reorganized Church of Jesus Christ of Latter Day Saints has continued to accept the active guidance and creative power of the Holy Spirit, it has set up certain criteria for determining what expressions are approved by the church as the mind and will of God.

1. While not necessarily essential, it is nevertheless expected that prophetic instruction to the church comes through the prophet of the church, who has been called to that office by the Holy Spirit.
2. Inspired instruction to the church is received and accepted by the common consent of the church met in a World Conference. It is the faith of the church that the Holy Spirit which inspires the one who presents the instruction as the mind of God also enlightens the membership to know the validity and truth of the instruction given.
3. The Holy Spirit functions in many ways throughout the church—in calling persons to priesthood or other responsibility, inspiring ministry, healing the sick, confirming the ordinances, and on occasion instructing persons—but these expressions are not to be recorded and circulated to people who were not present during the initial experience.

The Present Dilemma

Unfortunately the policies of the church against writing, recording, or circulating material which claims to be inspired but which has not received the confirming judgment of common consent are not always followed.

The elements of magic which are always at hand cloud the use of the gifts and cheapen the meaning of spiritual experience. The hope of receiving personal acclaim or achieving personal ambitions through attributing one's desires to the Holy Spirit is still present. Ascribing statements of little-known persons to well-known church leaders still occurs.

The church faces the embarrassment of the misuse or the spurious use of that which claims to be the inspiration of the Holy Spirit. People are still confused and torn between the elements of magic and genuine spiritual manifestations.

In Conclusion

The expression of that which is falsely claimed to be the Holy Spirit has been the greatest enemy of the free exercise of the Spirit. It is in essence the age-old tension between self-centered magic which seeks to control all the forces of the universe and genuine spiritual experience which urges one to yield one's self to God and become fully aligned with his purposes.

The church has always struggled with this tension. Its tendency has been to so limit the expressions of the Holy Spirit which it will accept that it loses the creative life which is the presence of the living Christ.

When this deadening effect has worked its course there has occurred from time to time a revitalization of the church and a resurgence of the Holy Spirit in the midst of the people.

An ever-present concern of the church is to keep the expressions of the Holy Spirit pure, free from the tarnish of selfish people who would use its power for self-serving ends. At the same time the church must be open to the dynamic action of God through the Holy Spirit. This is a tension which defies simple answers.

STUDY HELPS

1. The author uses the term *embarrassment* in speaking of the difficulties of the early disciples. What does the word mean? How has your personal use been consistent with the author's views? Inconsistent?
2. What are some of the idols of today's society? Which ones are important to you? Why? To what extent must these idols die in order for Christ to live in your heart? Why?
3. What was the underlying value of the decisions of the Council of Trent (1545–1563)? How did it strengthen the scriptures? Weaken them? What may be its long-term effect as every effort is made to keep magic out of the expressions of the Holy Spirit?
4. You and several other students may like to read chapter 15 in *Exploring the Faith.* What is the nature of revelation? How does response to it occur? How is your understanding similar to or different from the author's?
5. In a very real way Joseph Smith faced the same embarrassment discussed by the author. How did Joseph deal with the question of individual "revelation"? How is it possible to make this distinction within ourselves?
6. Give your personal definition of *revelation.* What is the contemporary church position on revelation? Make a list and compare the differences, expectations, and audience when an individual is moved by the Spirit to speak compared to when the prophet of the church speaks.
7. What does *ex cathedra* mean? How did this occur in the church? There is considerable difference between the *ex cathedra* speaking of the pope and the speaking of the prophet. What are several of the major differences?

CHAPTER 17

THE MEANING OF SALVATION

The angelic messengers announced to the shepherds of Judea that Jesus Christ was born, and declared him to be a Savior: "For unto you is born this day, in the city of David, a Savior, who is Christ the Lord" (Luke 2:11). For Christians the idea of Jesus as Savior is central to their faith.

Christians are not alone in believing in salvation. Other religions have beliefs about salvation and the ways this can be achieved. For the Buddhist, salvation means achieving Nirvana or a state of "passionless peace"—perhaps even individual annihilation in which people are freed from the round of rebirths which subject them to the pain and evil of life here on earth. For the Moslem, salvation is otherworldly and is primarily concerned with escape from the judgment of Allah. This can be achieved by works, including performing the five or six obligations that are expected of all Moslems, and belief in the oneness of Allah, Mohammed as his prophet, the Koran, divine judgment, and in angels.

Christianity, like other religious faiths, has had various emphases in its teachings about salvation. In a general way, the ideas about salvation have been determined by the evils or negatives from which people felt they needed to be saved. The ultimate negative is spiritual death or exclusion from eternal life. In this sense salvation has to do with the eternal consequences which result from this life.

In the early Christian churches of Greece, error and death were the evils from which people believed they needed to be saved. The Roman Catholic Church asserted that people needed to be saved from guilt and the consequence of guilt. The classical Protestant churches supported the need to be saved from "the law" and the "works of the law" with its resulting anxiety and condemnation. In liberal Protestantism the elimination of certain sins and progress toward moral perfection were the essence of salvation. Latter Day Saints consider the Zionic call to achieve a godly society to be involved in salvation. They believe society must be redeemed as well as individuals within it.

Salvation, then, has been generally perceived as the positive answer to the evils which people have seen as the most destructive or feared consequences of life. Ideas of salvation have changed as people's suffering, fears, and hungers have shifted. When persons were bound by poverty and hunger, salvation envisioned "streets of gold." When people were burdened by labor, salvation involved leisure and the time to "strum a harp." Some American Indians thought of salvation as a "happy hunting ground."

Salvation as Healing

While Christians have held varying views of salvation the original meaning may be better understood from its root word *salvus* which means *healed*. When salvation is interpreted as healing, it relates to the Christian understanding of the human predicament in which estrangement is the universal plight. The healing implied in salvation is the reuniting of humankind with God, of person with person, of persons with the universe, and persons with themselves.

Salvation is the work of Christ within persons to redeem or reclaim them from the fragmented and estranged circumstances of existence. It brings about within persons a new birth in which the conflicting issues which cause the estrangement are resolved through a new allegiance in Christ. While this aspect of the healing and saving power of Jesus is seen all through the meaning of Christ in our redemption, there is a special way in which this power is experienced in the sacrament of the Lord's Supper. Christ himself was both the model of that new being and the source of power through which each one may become a new being. This gives significance to the descriptive term *redeemer* as one who reclaims people from the circumstance of their estrangement in the temporal universe and calls them to the unity and wholeness of sons and daughters of God. The author of the Ephesian letter wrote:

> But now, in Christ Jesus, ye who sometimes were far off are made nigh by the blood of Christ. For he is our peace, who hath made both one, and hath broken down the middle wall of partition between us; having abolished in his flesh the enmity, even the law of commandments contained in ordinances; for to make in himself of twain one new man, so making peace; and that he might reconcile both unto God in one body by the cross, having slain the enmity thereby; and came and preached peace to you which were afar off, and to them that were nigh.—Ephesians 2:13-17

Our Christian faith confronts us with God's creative action which has brought us into the temporal universe. God knew full well the estrangement would be experienced and committed himself to pay the price to lead us through the predicament. If we will let God, he will empower us to be reunited with the eternal in a new creation in Christ. This is rightly understood as salvation.

Salvation for All

Fortunately this salvation is not for a favored few. The idea of salvation being limited to a special group or even to all who profess Christ in this life is not a biblical teaching. Salvation is the divine healing extended by God's sacrificial action to all. The Jews had to learn that salvation was also for the Gentiles. Saints must learn that salvation is also extended to those not of the Restoration faith. The righteous and self-righteous must know that salvation is for the scoundrel as well as for them. The healing power of God's action through Jesus Christ has no limits except as persons refuse to accept his love or allow his Spirit to work in them.

Human estrangement is not a matter of God being estranged from humanity. The atonement is not a price paid by God through Christ to assuage his own wrath. Rather, it is the price paid to enable people to accept the gift of God's grace and be reconciled to him. Divine initiative is taken to empower persons to break the shackles of sin and become the sons and daughters of God. God accepts the unfathomable cost to reconcile the human race to him. It is paid not for a few but for all. The scriptures have noted

> that at the name of Jesus every knee should bow, of things in heaven, and things in earth, and things under the earth; and that every tongue should confess that Jesus Christ is Lord, to the glory of God the Father.—Philippians 2:10, 11

Obviously, not all people hear or know of Jesus Christ in this life and it would be presumptuous of the church to detail the means by which God accomplishes his saving and healing work. Nevertheless, both the sense of God's love and justice and the scriptures give us the assurance that God in his own way extends the ministry of his Spirit to all people:

> For as the Father hath life in himself, so hath he given to the Son to have life in himself; and hath given him authority to execute judgment also, because he is the Son of Man. Marvel not at this; for the hour is coming, in the which all who are in their graves shall hear his voice, and shall come forth; they who have done good, in the resurrection of the just; and they who have done evil, in the resurrection of the unjust.—John 5:26-29

The book of I Peter contains the account of Christ preaching to the "spirits in prison; some of whom were disobedient in the days of Noah" and later states, "Because of this, is the gospel preached to them who are dead, that they might be judged according to men in the flesh, but live in the spirit according to the will of God" (I Peter 3:19, 20; 4:6). While there are many questions about the extent and nature of life beyond present temporal existence, we are assured that the love, grace, and justice of God are extended to all who will receive his gift of eternal life and affirmatively live in the spirit and nature of the new being in Christ.

Grace and Works

Salvation is the gift of God to all people and is possible because of God's unfathomable love when entering into his own creation through Jesus Christ. The amazing grace of God guarantees his love and acceptance even when we fail to measure up to the standards of perfection. We do not assume, however, that the person's own response is unimportant. Too long Christians have argued the relative significance of God's grace as opposed to human works as if these were antagonists rather than essential elements of salvation.

Salvation, like life itself, is a gift from God and is received not as a deserved possession which is earned but as an unmerited gift of love. Also, God cannot give his gifts to those who reject him. Just as one person cannot receive the love of another person without responding affirmatively to that love, so persons cannot receive the love of God and the gift of eternal life without affirmatively responding to God. While the grace of God guarantees that his arms are open to all, intentional affirmative response and the giving of ourselves in loving service to God are required if we are to receive his gifts. Salvation is not extrinsic to the person. We do not put on salvation like a coat or pair of shoes. Salvation is like spiritual and intellectual growth. It is intrinsic. We become the sons and daughters of God and participate in eternal life as we respond to God's love by loving him and actively living our lives in service and for God's purposes. This is recognition that our lives and all that we influence are of divine creation and therefore sacred. Our calling is to be actively engaged with God in fulfilling his purposes. We use or develop God's gifts as a stewardship, fully aware that we are God's and that we are only accountable to the Father.

In the giving of ourselves in sacrificial service we are remade in the image and likeness of the eternal and are saved. This is not due to personal efforts to gain salvation but rather to devoted response to God's grace.

The Process of Salvation

Although God acts in myriad ways and each person's experience in conversion is different, most of us recognize that we have gone through a conversion process. In this life we cannot say at any one time, "I am now fully reborn as a son or daughter of God." As we live and serve in the climate of the Holy Spirit we develop new dimensions of personality, greater understanding of God and his purposes in us, and deeper appreciation of his love and abundant provision for his creation. Life becomes increasingly radiant and salvation expands in meaning and significance.

Generally that conversion process includes the following steps in growth:

1. Becoming aware of our human predicament with its conflicting values, tensions, anxieties, and self-centered motives. We must be conscious of the need for something better. This may come from association with those whose lives help us see our own estrangement, from hearing the gospel preached,

experiencing worship, or from some traumatic event such as a narrow escape from death or the loss of a close friend.

2. Becoming aware that we do not have the power of our own selves to escape our predicament. We may try fads, social movements, and the latest psychological thought patterns, only to find them inadequate. These will not heal our estrangement at the deeper levels of life.

3. Experiencing some degree of despair as we recognize our own powerlessness. This may lead to the disposition to give up because life seems futile.

4. Experiencing humility and repentance. In the midst of discovering that we are not strong enough, good enough, or wise enough to save ourselves, we may then come to accept ourselves as we really are and ask for help. In this stage we may desire to become what we sense to be good and fulfilling. This is the longing to be rid of the destructive life we have experienced and to lay hold of that which is fruitful, lasting, and fulfilling. It is the desire to be morally and spiritually healed. Affirmatively recognized, it is the search for God's grace and the "thirst after righteousness."

5. Willingness to turn loose of the past and by a leap of faith grasp the best that we can honestly believe about the nature of life, the nature of God, and the intent of God for humanity. In this experience we feel the call of God and respond in faith, willing to yield ourselves to him. This is symbolized and consummated in baptism.

6. Continued life in the community of the church where, through fellowship with others who have committed themselves to God, through worship where the Holy Spirit is experienced, and through service in stewardship, the process of salvation continues in

each of us. Many who have lived in this process say we have been and are being saved.

In Conclusion

The Christian doctrine of salvation is central to our belief and is real in experience. Salvation is experienced in the process of growth which takes place within us through conversion, commitment, and loving service to God. The Holy Spirit works salvation in us when with all our hearts we want to serve God and make of our lives a stewardship.

Like so many things in life, salvation is achieved not so much by a preoccupation with seeking salvation as it is a consequence of serving God.

STUDY HELPS

1. Salvation comes from the word that means healed. What does it mean to be healed of sin? How is this a statement about human innocence? Human resurrections? Why? Review the previous chapter and consider your answers.
2. Read chapter 16 of *Exploring the Faith* and report about the role of scriptures in understanding salvation. How is this view similar to yours? Different?
3. The author points out that the great redeeming value of the love of God is that God loves people because of who he is, not because of who they are. What does this tell about the meaning of human estrangement? What is the model it sets for all to follow? How does the story of the adulterous woman illustrate this model?
4. What may be some reasons why the author sees no conflict between grace and works? What is your

definition of grace? Works? How have Latter Day Saints stressed works? How is this balanced by grace?

5. Restate the six points of the conversion process. How are these similar or different from your experience? How may you still be in the process of conversion? What additional steps would you add? Why?
6. How does "Arise from the dust, my sons, and be men" (Book of Mormon, II Nephi 1:36) relate to the process of conversion? Describe to another student or a friend your conversion experience or one of a friend. How are yours similar to other people's? Different?
7. How do you react to the author's assertion that salvation is for all? Does this mean that everyone will be saved? Why or why not?

CHAPTER

THE POWER OF ETERNAL JUDGMENT

The principle of eternal judgment takes the "milk toast" of sentimentality out of Christian faith. God's love and grace have unfortunately sometimes been interpreted by modern people as if God were a permissive and sentimental old man who always rushes out to assure people that they are forgiven even when their repentance is feigned or commitment shallow and self-serving. Facing up to the fact that we are all accountable to God for what we do and become is a sobering experience. Yet we need not be fearful. Some have pictured judgment as negative, involving dread of being confronted by personal sin and failures. Surely everyone is all too conscious of those negative elements, but life has its positive elements too. We have also cultivated God's gifts in good ways and exercised effective stewardship management. Eternal judgment reveals the good as well as the bad, the glory as well as the condemnation.

There is instruction given to the church: "The church is admonished again that joint responsibility is laid on all. Properly and equally borne, this responsibility will insure success, the consummation will be glorious, and all will share in that glory" (Doctrine and Covenants 141:8). Eternal judgment opens our lives to joy as well as remorse.

Life is a mixture of the noble and the petty, the courageous and the cowardly, the good done and the good withheld. Most of us have read such scriptures as

Matthew 25:32-47, and have been aware that we have sometimes fed the hungry, helped clothe the naked, and visited the sick and those in prison. We take our place with the sheep until we recall the many times we should have helped those in need but chose not to get involved or give of our means or energy for another. We know we belong with the goats as well as the sheep. Our human judgment can never unravel the complexities of life.

The Futility of Weighing Good and Evil

This impossible task of trying to weigh the good works which we do against the evil or sinful acts always confronts us with a destructive dilemma. We often focus on the evil, seeing it in a true measure of its awfulness and cost both to God and his creation. This cannot be done without sensing the forgiving grace of God, and feeling that we are undone and overwhelmed by the magnitude of the evil.

At this point we must each come to grips with the fact that God did not create us as gods; he created us as humans and expects us to be human. Christ has come to be the New Creation in the midst of humanity. We are being lifted up to become new beings in him. We lay down the burden of our sin and failure and go free as forgiven children when we confess our sin and failure, repent, and earnestly ask God's help and forgiveness. The sacraments are of particular assistance at this point.

Becoming preoccupied with weighing personal good works against the bad leads people to self-righteousness and Pharisaism. Many times we focus on a list of sins we have eliminated from our lives and on the good works we have done. While comparing ourselves with other people we feel more righteous than they and become judgmental of others. We begin to think of ourselves more highly than we ought and become more harsh in our evaluation of other people. We must recognize that personal vanity and lack of compassion are deadly.

The Awfulness of Sin

The cost of sin as experienced in hatred, human rebellion, pride, selfishness, and exploitation is grievous to God. We are told that because of this, "the heavens weep" (Genesis 7:35). Such sin is the source of the world's greatest tragedy. It brings conflicts of purpose within the sinner, between persons, and between persons and God. Sin destroys harmony and disrupts reconciliation. Eternal judgment is evident in the results of sin and in the internal nature of sin itself. The scriptures point out that "the wages of sin is death" (Romans 6:23).

Sin and the Person

The presumption that God condemns sin but not the sinner is superficial and false. Sin is not something separate from the person. The awesome fact is that God still loves us and tries to entice us from sin to repentance. This is seen in the anguish of Christ as he wept over Jerusalem (Matthew 23:36-38). The universal character of sin causes God the pain of crucifixion daily.

When we consider the effect of human pride, lust, greed, and thirst for power, we are aware of the enormous cost in war, crime, fraud, addiction to alcohol and drugs, racial and class persecution, tyranny, and human cruelty. The staggering consequences of sin cannot be sloughed over in any easygoing way as if God, because of his love, does not hold people accountable. The consequences for both the sinner and the innocent are evident in the nature of life. Sin destroys.

The Eternal Character of Sin

Divine judgment on the world is a scriptural concept. It is part of the eternal nature of God. The Creator who brings the universe into existence, and creates persons in his own image, has purpose in his acts. That purpose is written in the nature of eternity. While many may feel that values are relative and that people make their own criteria for good and evil, in the long run such thoughts and actions fail.

If moral laws were determined by people there would be no sin in the scriptural sense. Sin is rebellion against divine command with its consequent estrangement from God. If moral law were a human invention, there could be no divine judgment. Without enduring moral law there could be no good or evil, right or wrong. We would be left to a moral relativism in which we each make our own truth by willing it to be true and then pressing that will on others by force. The world's very existence would be threatened. Such a state of affairs sometimes seems to govern until the sanity of divine judgment asserts itself again.

Eternal Judgment as God's Judgment

In its more personal sense eternal judgment is God's judgment. It is experienced by persons who, through the impress of the Holy Spirit, come to see life and the circumstances of life as they really are. In some measure it is seeing through the eyes of God; therefore, in its finest expression, eternal judgment is a function of worship. The things we consider important, the goals for which we work, the ways we spend our time and resources become so distorted in this life that we waste our time, resources, and lives. We indulge in hatred, social climbing, jockeying for professional status, and a host of other objectives which seem desirable, until in worship many experience the gift of eternal judgment.

Under this Spirit we suddenly see the froth and chaff of some of the things we have considered important. Things which are good and lasting and of eternal value are understood to be of real worth. The awfulness of sin is revealed and the glory and richness of life with Christ are disclosed. This is the principle of eternal judgment. Those who are led by the Holy Spirit experience it. Judgment is a gift of the Spirit symbolized in confirmation by the laying on of hands, through which those who have committed their lives to Christ are promised the abiding Comforter. The Comforter abides with those who involve themselves daily in worship through prayer, study of the scriptures, participation in the services of the church (particularly the sacraments), and in steady, faithful stewardship as they manage their resources.

The Dimensions of Eternal Judgment

In its deeper dimensions eternal judgment opens our vision to understand the profound, everlasting, and wide-ranging effects of every act and every thought and every attitude we harbor. Under the impress of the Holy Spirit we see the implications of what we cultivate within ourselves. We understand what these things do to us, but we also understand what we do to others for both good and bad. Under the spirit of eternal judgment we know that what we do to others changes their lives and causes them to influence persons around them. This chain of effect passes from one to another until it influences multitudes of people. Our actions not only influence those living persons far and wide but also affect their children and ongoing generations. We readily accept this fact when we realize that the lives of great men and women of former years live on in us. We stand on the shoulders of the Isaiahs, Florence Nightingales, Abraham Lincolns, Frederick M. Smiths, and Winston

Churchills of the past. We also are influenced by the Jezebels, King Noahs, Hitlers, and Idi Amins of history. We come to see in eternal judgment under the impress of the Holy Spirit that we are all linked together in the human race. We may not be identified and remembered as are those who have made some specific contribution that has grasped the attention of history, but our influence is there too.

The Offer of New Beginnings

As indicated previously, under the spirit of eternal judgment, we are aware of good and noble influences, but all of us have done those things which were sinful and destructive to ourselves and to others. The weight of eternal judgment would be crushing if it were not for the provisions God has made for us to lay the burden down, especially through the ordinances, and be assured of God's forgiving grace. Through this provision we can go free from the weight and bondage of guilt to become what under the Spirit we sense God is calling us to be.

We are required to go to those we have injured and ask to be forgiven and reconciled. We are also required to forgive and open our hearts to the reconciling power of the Holy Spirit before we go to God to ask for our burden to be removed. Jesus taught his disciples to pray: "Forgive us our trespasses, as we forgive those who trespass against us" (Matthew 6:13). That is a sobering thought when we realize how often we have been unforgiving.

The Final Judgment

The principle of eternal judgment includes the Christian belief in a final judgment as the scriptures suggest in such passages as Revelation 20:11-15. The scriptures give symbols of the judgment involved at the end of time. Since this leads into the eternal and beyond the temporal world, it must be approached with a great deal of humility.

Clearly God does not need to wait until the "books are opened" to know what we have done or what kind of person we have become. Perhaps some must await a final judgment before they can understand the full meaning of the judgment of God on their lives.

Although the end of time is beyond human comprehension, the implications of our actions or "works" are an important factor in eternal judgment. It also has been the faith of the Saints through the years that the judgment is influenced by the degree of understanding and the opportunities afforded persons in life. Judgment considers the circumstances in which persons lived and the kind of persons they have become.

The Justice of Judgment

The Apostle Paul was aware that people may not fully understand or describe the nature of the judgment or its effect on the resurrection of persons. He wrote of the resurrection:

> That which thou sowest, thou sowest not that body which shall be, but grain, it may be of wheat, or some other; but God giveth it a body as it hath pleased him, and to every seed his own body. All flesh is not the same flesh; but there is one kind of flesh of men, another flesh of beasts, another of fishes, and another of birds. Also celestial bodies, and bodies terrestrial, and bodies telestial; but the glory of the celestial, one; and the terrestrial, another; and the telestial, another. There is one glory of the sun, and another glory of the moon, and another glory of the stars; for one star differeth from another star in glory. So also is the resurrection of the dead.—I Corinthians 15:37-42

Obviously much of the preceding scripture illustrates how Christians need not fret about their resurrection and future state. The same eternal principles and power by which God orders the unfathomable gift of life assures us that he will keep his promises. The illustration of the glories reminds us of God's justice and love which grant to all people that state in the future resurrection for which they are prepared. We must be careful not to presume a compartmentalization of the glories which includes an endless heaven or hell into which one might be plunged for eternity on the basis of a slight difference in the tipping of the scales of justice. The scripture sets out the principle in which God grants to us all the measure of glory for which we are prepared.

In Conclusion

While the final judgment presumes an accounting and disposition at the end of time, it is not different in kind from the other expressions of the principles of eternal judgment. God's judgment, experienced under the power of the Holy Spirit, may be seen symbolically by people through the eyes of God. In doing so we find the meaning of righteousness and of evil.

In this life we experience eternal judgment only in fragments, while in a final judgment we will see the total. Paul also wrote, "For now we see through a glass, darkly; but then face to face; now I know in part; but then shall I know even as also I am known" (I Corinthians 13:12). This, however, is a matter of degree and not kind. The principle of eternal judgment is not alone an event, important as an event may be. This continuing principle enables the follower of Christ to experience the power of the Holy Spirit as well as discern that which is right, good, and holy from that which is wrong, evil, and destructive. Eternal judgment is the power of God leading all persons to salvation.

STUDY HELPS

1. Eternal judgment is sometimes seen as that which follows death and reflects on all life beyond. How is judgment eternal? How has it begun already? Why or why not? How is eternal judgment made and seen by you? How are your views similar to the author's? Different?
2. Why do Christians tend to see eternal judgment in a negative way? Describe this principle in a positive manner.
3. Read Matthew 25:32-47. What is your response to this scripture? Why?
4. Why do most persons want eternal judgment? What are the points at which persons are judged? Who is involved in this judging? When have you felt judged? Why?
5. How does God's judgment mean that personal failures, even sinfulness, are forever condemned? How does this chapter on judgment compare with the earlier chapter on healing. How can there be one without the other? Why?
6. What does the legal use of the word *judgment* mean? How is the scriptural use similar to or different from the legal definition?
7. Read Elton Trueblood's *Confronting Christ* (Harper and Row, 1960), chapter 52, "The Ecclesiastical Court." This may be summarized and reported back to your class. How do you agree or disagree with Trueblood? Why?

CHAPTER 19

THE END OF TIME

Matthew's account of Jesus' final appearance ends with these words to the disciples: "Be assured, I am with you always, to the end of time" (Matthew 28:19 NEB). As mortals it is very difficult for us to deal with such a concept as "the end of time." We use symbols and allegories, but are unable to give any literal details of such future history.

By affirming that God is the creator of all that exists, we acknowledge that the universe of time and space had a beginning. It was created and is therefore temporal as contrasted with eternal. In a symbolic way we may say the universe emerged from and exists within the "bosom of eternity."

Since the universe of time and space was created by God and had a beginning, Christians have faith that God has invested his purposes in that creation. The creation is temporal or temporary as it relates to the eternal.

> The Lord God spake unto Moses, saying, The heavens, they are many and they can not be numbered unto man, but they are numbered unto me, for they are mine; and as one earth shall pass away, and the heavens thereof, even so shall another come; and there is no end to my works, neither to my words; for this is my work and my glory, to bring to pass the immortality, and eternal life of man.—Doctrine and Covenants 22:23

God's purposes in his creation will be fulfilled and the temporal subsumed in the culmination of this time and space existence. Again, in a symbolic way, the scriptures speak of that condition in which a new heaven and a new earth shall be (Revelation 21:1).

As distinguished from the temporal universe which has a beginning and an end, God is eternal. The New Testament refers to God as "Alpha and Omega, the beginning and the end" (Revelation 21:6). This gives us to understand that God, as the creator of time and space, is the source within which all time exists. The temporal universe may end, but God does not.

The Significance of the Beginning and the End

The concept of a beginning and an end to the temporal creation is crucially significant to our faith. It is the frame in which we derive a sense of meaning for history, personal relationships, and the purposes of God. We live our lives in light of our understanding of the beginning and the end. We believe that those purposes are revealed and guaranteed in Jesus Christ.

Christians understand that God's creative action in bringing into existence the temporal universe has been widely proclaimed. They affirm that God is the creator of all that exists and has created it for his own purposes. We are assured that all creation is sacred and has been affirmed by God to be good. For this reason we can believe that God is omnipotent. God cannot do everything we can conjure up in our imagination, but rather God is ultimately the source of all that exists. All is under his control and judgment. God is the only ultimate source of power or intelligence. All existence is invested with the divine intention to fulfill the purposes of God, and when it does not contribute to God's intent it goes against its own nature and must eventually destroy itself.

The other side of history is viewed from the concept of the end of time. This is the meaning of *Omega*, the culmination of history when the purposes written into creation will be fulfilled because God is the creator. While the concepts of the end always stagger the human mind and must be expressed in symbols rather than in any literal description, the symbols are tremendously valuable. They help us deal with that which is beyond concrete experience.

Just as the concepts of the beginning of time give us a basis for belief in the nature, purpose, and sacredness of creation, so our concepts of the end toward which creation moves reinforce our understanding of our own existence. They give purpose and a point of direction for ordering our lives. We do not dwell on our own death or become preoccupied with the end of time. Nevertheless, a keen awareness of the end of this short existence as it relates to the fulfillment of God's purposes gives us discernment in viewing life's values, and serenity in confronting the demands life makes on us. That which may be seen only as tragedy by one without a sense of eternal destiny, may be viewed calmly as but the prologue to victory by one whose understanding of the fulfillment of time is rooted in the Christian faith. The temptations to live this life for the moment are put in perspective when seen in terms of their eternal dimensions.

The End of History as Revealed in Jesus

The essential Christian understanding of the end toward which history moves is revealed in Jesus Christ. He is the new being, the new creation, which is the model and prophecy of the fulfillment of God's purposes in humanity and history. Christ is the evidence of the power by which God shall fulfill his purposes. He is the tangible assurance of those divine promises. Christians confidently live to fulfill these promises because they are revealed in him.

While we cannot fully explore the meaning of Christ's revelation, it is appropriate to mention four central understandings revealed in Christ.

First, Jesus taught and revealed in his own life the

divine purpose in the kingdom of God. This was not limited to some spiritual kingdom beyond this life; he spoke of the kingdom of God on earth. He taught his disciples to pray, "Thy kingdom come. Thy will be done on earth, as it is done in heaven" (Matthew 6:11). The numerous scriptural references to Jesus "preaching the gospel of the kingdom" give ample evidence of the primacy of this theme in his ministry. Jesus Christ gives ample testimony to God's intent that persons will fulfill their calling to become the new beings which he revealed. When the apostle wrote, "God is in Christ, reconciling the world unto himself" (II Corinthians 5:19), he was expressing the role of Christ out of which the kingdom of God emerges. The kingdom of God is the product of reconciled and redeemed persons as they live out the principles of the gospel in everyday life. There are many other scriptural writings and terms which symbolize the idea of eventual reconciliation as characteristic of the kingdom. The statement in Isaiah 11:5-9 forecasts an unprecedented reconciliation of creation. The idea of the millennium gives symbols of God's intention for the end of time. These symbols are valuable, but like other symbols of that which is beyond our might, we must be humble in our conclusions about them and remember that they give visions of hope, not literal descriptions of the culmination of time.

Second, Jesus reveals the intention and power of the Resurrection. While the revelation found in Christ assures us of God's intent and power to provide for his creation, we must not assume we know the details of that which is unknowable. Like the early Christians, we believe that "it doth not yet appear what we shall be; but we know that, when he shall appear, we shall be like him; for we shall see him as he is" (I John 3:2). Nevertheless, our confidence in the Resurrection gives assurance of God's intention for us and all of creation.

The Resurrection gives meaning to life and hope which could not have been except for Christ's revelation.

Third, Christ reveals the holiness, mercy, and justice of God's purpose in creation. In our short span of existence in this temporal world it is easy to be confused by temporary experiences. Cruelty goes unpunished, the weak are trodden down, criminals succeed, and the innocent suffer. The injustice of war sickens us and the unfairness of government's best-made laws bewilders us. We are swayed by our own desires and the expectations of our companions. Jesus Christ revealed in his life and in his teachings the love, holiness, and justice of God. The idea of eternal judgment assures us of the ultimate justice in all things. We feel assured that in the end righteousness, justice, and virtue will take their rightful place.

Fourth, Christ assures us that the ultimate purposes and promises of God are guaranteed. The victory is already won because God is God. We do not watch history unfold in fear, wondering what the outcome will be. We already know. We have read the last chapter of the book of history and now see the intermediate plot unfold. We are not dismayed but rejoice in the fulfillment of history. This is not to say that we avoid suffering or that the world escapes being engulfed in the struggle between evil and righteousness. Rather we declare that the struggle is not in vain nor the outcome ultimately in doubt.

Witnesses to the Truth Revealed in Christ

The scriptures are a way by which the meaning of Christ's revelation is transmitted to each generation; they are therefore very important to us. The scriptures testify of Christ, and although they are not the only source of that revelation, they are a valuable one.

The church itself is the continuing community in

which that revelation in Christ resides and is witnessed to the world. Christ lives on in the church.

The Holy Spirit is the power and presence of the living Christ which opens our understanding to the meaning of the "word made flesh" in him. We experience this in worship and inspiration. The Spirit enables us to have faith and empowers us to commit ourselves to Christ.

All of these, and any other power or intelligence which the world receives, is but a part of, or a footnote to, the revelation already given in the Lord Jesus. These witnesses may deepen our understanding and bring new dimensions to our response to God's revelation in Christ, the "fullness of the gospel." The scriptures confirm this:

> And this is the gospel, the glad tidings which the voice out of the heavens bore record unto us, that he came into the world, even Jesus to be crucified for the world, and to bear the sins of the world, and to sanctify the world, and to cleanse it from all unrighteousness.—Doctrine and Covenants 76:4g

The Role of Apocalypse

With this understanding of the meaning of Christ to all generations we approach apocalyptic writings about the end of time with a central reference for judging and interpreting them. We ought not, however, become preoccupied with the apocalyptic writings as if they were new revelation. When soberly understood, such writings of history's end are a confirmation of the prophetic revelation of Jesus and the assurance that his promises will come to pass.

Perhaps the best example of this fact is the theme and purpose of the book of Revelation. Much of the book is allegory understood by the saints of the first century but unintelligible to their enemies. While the book does confirm the prophecy written into Christ's revelation, its primary thrust was to encourage the disciples, in their time of great persecution, to remain faithful and endure to the end. The central theme was a message to the churches in Asia to be faithful, for God's purposes will be fulfilled: "He that hath an ear, let him hear what the Spirit saith unto the churches; To him that overcometh will I give to eat of the tree of life, which is in the midst of the paradise of God" (Revelation 2:7). The writer urged the saints to persevere. He was not trying to give them inside mysteries about the future which Christ had somehow neglected to reveal.

In Conclusion

When we proclaim a beginning to the temporal universe we reasonably assume an end. We ought not try to place specific limits on either. Many today are coming to understand that the beginning of creation is measured in eons and the universe is much older than once imagined. The important affirmation for Christian faith is not when or how creation took place but that God was in the beginning. God is the creator.

The end of time is also unknown to us and has already been much later than the early disciples expected. No one knows when God will fulfill his purposes in creation, but we have faith that they will be fulfilled. The promise of God is: "I am the Beginning and the End" (Genesis 1:2).

We are not priviliged to know the ending time nor the details of the future. These are beyond our ability as humans in the temporal world to fully comprehend because of the eternal implications of the end time. In Christ, however, we have the revelation of God's nature and intent. God's purpose for all creation including the human race is graphically illustrated. We have assurance that the kingdom of God, in which the purposes of God are fulfilled in time, will be. For the faithful Christian, the affirmation is in every age: "To him that overcometh will I give to eat of the tree of life, which is in the midst of the paradise of God" (Revelation 2:7).

STUDY HELPS

1. What is the meaning of the word *eschatology*? Which books of the Bible are eschatological? Why is a sense of eschatology necessary for a sense of meaning in history?
2. What is the role of agency in understanding a statement like "This [the end] is the culmination of history when the purposes written into creation from the beginning will be fulfilled because God is the Creator." How does agency work?
3. Read Isaiah 11:5-9. What two events are forecast? Why was this shared by the Old Testament writers? How does this scripture speak to present-day society?
4. What are the four central understandings of the revelation of Christ in light of previous chapters? What would you add to this list? How is there yet more light to bear on God's revelation? Why? What remains for people to be told other than the commandments they have now been given? What are people's most basic needs? How does God relate to these needs?
5. You or another student may like to read chapter 19 in *Exploring the Faith*. Prepare a panel presentation covering various elements of this belief statement.
6. The consideration of last things has occupied persons since the beginning of written history. Why is the concern for "end" so wrapped up in ethics? Make a list of your major ethical concerns. How may a change in your understanding of "the end" alter your behavior? Why?
7. Ethics is a human response to the necessity of laws. The character of your response to revelation is bound to affect how you understand ethics. Why must there be personal obligations to respond to revelation, assuming that revelation is the commitment of God, through Jesus Christ, to his people?